Decolonization: A Very Short Introduction

VERY SHORT INTRODUCTIONS are for anyone wanting a stimulating and accessible way into a new subject. They are written by experts, and have been translated into more than 40 different languages.

The series began in 1995, and now covers a wide variety of topics in every discipline. The VSI library now contains over 450 volumes—a Very Short Introduction to everything from Indian philosophy to psychology and American history and relativity—and continues to grow in every subject area.

Very Short Introductions available now:

Available soon:

For more information visit our web site

www.oup.com/vsi/

Dane Kennedy

DECOLONIZATION

A Very Short Introduction

OXFORD

UNIVERSITY PRESS

Oxford University Press is a department of the University of Oxford.
It furthers the University's objective of excellence in research, scholarship,
and education by publishing worldwide. Oxford is a registered trade mark of
Oxford University Press in the UK and certain other countries.

Published in the United States of America by Oxford University Press
198 Madison Avenue, New York, NY 10016, United States of America

Library of Congress Cataloging-in-Publication Data
Kennedy, Dane Keith.
Decolonization : a very short introduction / Dane Kennedy.
pages cm
Includes bibliographical references and index.
ISBN 978-0-19-934049-1 (pbk. : alk. paper)
1. Decolonization—History.   I. Title.
JV151.K46   2016
325'.3—dc23
2015030023

Printed by Integrated Books International, United States of America
on acid-free paper

*For the 150 alumni of the International
Decolonization Seminar*

Contents

List of illustrations

Acknowledgments

I want to thank Shawn McHale and Jason Parker, along with Jennifer Foray and Michael Collins (who read the manuscript for the press), for their exceedingly helpful comments. They saved me countless errors of fact and focus. A special word of gratitude goes to Wm. Roger Louis, who invited me to join the faculty of the inaugural International Decolonization Seminar in 2006 and whose own scholarship has done so much to shape our understanding of decolonization. He and the other seminar leaders—Philippa Levine, Jason Parker, Pillarisetti Sudhir, and Marilyn Young, along with guest faculty members Jennifer Foray and Lori Watt—have taught me a great deal. But my greatest debt goes to the 150 early-career scholars who have passed through the seminar over the past decade. It has been my great good fortune to meet and learn from these talented individuals, who came from a wide range of countries and brought a rich abundance of experiences, insights, and knowledge to the seminar. This book is dedicated to them.

Introduction

The United Nations has grown from 51 member states at its
founding in 1945 to 193 today. The vast majority of the new states
admitted over this period came into existence as a result of the
collapse of European imperial regimes. They are the products of a
historic shift from a world of colonial empires to a world of
nation-states. Although empires of other sorts arguably endure
and exert continued influence on global affairs, they are obliged to
operate within an international system that privileges the
nation-state, with its claim to territorial integrity and sovereignty,
along with the premise that that sovereignty derives in some
fashion from "the people." What this modern international system
has deemed unacceptable is colonialism: the imposition by a
foreign power of direct rule over another people. This position was
affirmed in a series of UN resolutions, culminating in Resolution
1514 of 1960, which denounced colonialism "as a serious abuse of
human rights" and declared that self-determination was "legally
binding." Such pronouncements point to a profoundly important
transformation in the international norms governing the
relationship between polities and peoples.

The tumultuous process that brought this transformation about
has come to be known as decolonization. This term appears to
have been coined in the early nineteenth century by a French
journalist who objected to his country's conquest of Algeria.

1

Others adopted its use over the next few decades, but it then disappeared from the political lexicon for nearly a century. Moritz Julius Bonn, a noted German Jewish social scientist who found refuge from the Nazis at the London School of Economics, is often credited with its resurrection in the 1930s. Even so, the term remained virtually unknown until the Second World War, and only after 1960 did it come into general usage.

The Oxford English Dictionary defines decolonization as the "withdrawal from its former colonies of a colonial power; the acquisition of political or economic independence by such colonies." The key words in that definition are "withdrawal" and "acquisition," terms that connote sober financial transactions carried out by mutual agreement. These associations are reinforced by the synonym to decolonization offered by the *OED*—"transfer," a noun that refers in legal parlance to the "conveyance from one person to another of property." Precisely such conveyances were carried out in a series of carefully choreographed independence ceremonies over several decades after World War II. Newsreel footage and still photographs give us a glimpse of these events: they show colonial officials and nationalist leaders standing on stages, giving speeches, signing documents, exchanging handshakes, and observing the lowering and raising of flags as bands played and crowds cheered. Such language and imagery has cast the collapse of empires and the rise of new nation-states in the decades after World War II as a consensual process, a peaceful transfer of sovereignty.

Nothing could have been farther from the truth: decolonization was a violent, fiercely contested process that pitted imperial rulers against colonial subjects. It also pitted anticolonial nationalists against one another. Yet the two parties whose representatives staged those ceremonial transfers of sovereignty both had reasons to minimize the turmoil and trauma that preceded the pomp and circumstance. For imperial states that were unable to keep colonial peoples under their control, it was obviously preferable to portray their loss of power as an act of altruism, the realization of

2

their long-standing claims that they were preparing their colonial charges for the responsibilities of self-government. But this was too often belied by the desperate determination with which they sought to cling to their colonies, manifested most notoriously in the ruthless counterinsurgency campaigns that cast such a long, dark shadow over the history of decolonization. When the violence and disorder that preceded the transfer of power prevented imperial authorities from claiming good will and gaining a graceful exit, they did their best to erase such unpleasantness from public memory through the destruction of documents and deliberate acts of forgetting.

The national regimes that replaced colonial authorities had their own reasons to promote selective amnesia about the upheavals that so often accompanied the transfer of power. Their official histories did, to be sure, celebrate the struggles that were required to win independence. They paid particular attention to the trials and tribulations of the new nations' founding fathers. But they also ignored or vilified those groups and individuals that had sought differently constituted states and notions of nationhood, not least because those efforts so often led to civil war and ethnic cleansing. Both imperial rulers and their heirs, then, shared an interest in promoting a selective and sanitized version of events, a version that presented it as a rational process carried out by political elites whose decisions affirmed the legitimacy of the governments they represented and the logic of the international system to which they claimed allegiance.

It is true that some colonies gained independence without incurring much violence. It is equally true that the prolonged and bloody campaigns against colonial rulers in places such as Algeria, Angola, Kenya, and Vietnam attracted much attention from contemporaries and continued to generate considerable scrutiny from historians and other scholars. Yet these cases have often been characterized as anomalies, exceptions to the broader pattern by which sovereignty was peacefully transferred to colonized peoples.

This perspective has been especially prevalent in Britain, which possessed the largest overseas empire. The former British prime minister Clement Attlee, for example, asserted in 1961 that Britain "has voluntarily surrendered its hegemony over subject peoples and has given them their freedom," doing so "without external pressure or weariness at the burden of ruling." Although some historians of the British Empire still endorse this view, portraying British decolonization as a carefully prepared, relatively peaceful process that avoided the pitfalls suffered by certain other imperial powers (notably France), research has shown that the British readily resorted to military force to maintain power over colonial subjects, retreating only when other options had been exhausted. In recent years, historians have turned their attention to the widespread violence that swept through British Asia during and after World War II, the terrible trauma that accompanied the partition of India, the brutal counterinsurgency campaign that incarcerated much of the Kikuyu population in Kenya, and the numerous other dismal episodes that punctuated the dying decades of the British Empire. And the stunning revelation that countless colonial documents detailing official crimes committed during the final years of British rule had been systematically destroyed and nearly nine thousand other politically embarrassing or legally incriminating files had been locked away for decades in a secret government archive at Hanslope Park confirmed a growing consensus that Britain was no less willing than other imperial states to employ any means necessary to maintain power.

If, then, decolonization is too bloodless and ideologically coded a term to adequately signify the scale of the turmoil and suffering that accompanied the collapse of the colonial empires after World War II, what other words are available to us? War? Revolution? Terror? While such terms fail to connote the historical specificity of the transformation that brought an end to colonial regimes, they all allude to certain aspects of its character that decolonization's transactional associations so signally fail to communicate. Furthermore, recognizing that war and revolution and terror were integral elements of these events permits us to place the story of the postwar disintegration of empires in a broader historical context. In particular, it directs our attention to earlier crises of empires and reveals certain patterns in their collapse that transcend some of the chronological and thematic divisions we conventionally employ in our accounts of the making of the contemporary world.

What we normally characterize as decolonization was the collapse of colonial empires and the creation of new nation-states across what came to be known in the decades following World War II as the Third World. Yet this upheaval was hardly unprecedented. Global clashes between empires had generated several prior waves of decolonization. The first occurred in the New World between 1776 and the 1820s, the second in the Old World between 1917 and the 1920s. The collapse of the Soviet Union after 1989 constituted, in turn, a fourth wave. Like the decolonization of the Third World, these other waves resulted in the fragmentation of some empires, the expansion and reconstitution of others, and the rise of new states—self-fashioned as nation-states to differentiate themselves from their ex-imperial overlords—in the spaces between empires.

Several important themes come into view when the decolonization of the Third World is set in the context of the two waves that preceded it, as well as the one that followed. The first is the crucial role that global wars between empires played in these events, creating the economic and political crises that gave colonized peoples the motives and opportunities to seek independence. A second theme concerns the options available to colonial rule's opponents: though the nation-state became the most commonly sought alternative, it was hardly the only one, and even its proponents often advanced conflicting visions of its composition. This leads in turn to our third theme, the widespread violence and frequent population transfers that accompanied so many of the struggles to forge new states from empires. Finally, this wider historical perspective permits us to see that the process of decolonization did not necessarily involve the rejection or negation of imperialism, nor did it cause empires to entirely disappear from the scene. More often than not, they simply reconstituted themselves in new forms.

This Very Short Introduction, while framed in the far broader chronological and geographical contexts that brought an end to colonial empires in the New and the Old Worlds, focuses on the decolonization of the Third World in the decades after World War II. This transformation took place in several phases that stretched from the mid-1940s through the late 1970s. The first phase happened in the immediate aftermath of World War II. It resulted in independence for Britain's South Asian possessions—India, Pakistan, Ceylon/Sri Lanka, and Burma/Myanmar—as well as the American Philippines and British and French-controlled territories in the Middle East, notably Palestine/Israel, Jordan, Lebanon, and Syria. A more far-reaching second phase began in the early 1950s and concluded in the late 1960s, by which point European colonial rule had collapsed across the rest of Asia (with the exception of Hong Kong), all of North Africa and most of sub-Saharan Africa (where more than thirty new nations came into existence), and much of the Caribbean. In the 1970s, a third phase of decolonization brought an end to the Portuguese empire in Africa and East Timor, the collapse of the renegade Rhodesian white regime, and independence to various Pacific island and Caribbean nations, along with a scattered array of other territories. The deluge that swept away the Western colonial empires would leave only a few random possessions—flotsam from the storm—in its wake by the end of the 1970s.

Though the last great wave of decolonization arguably occurred with the dissolution of the Soviet Union in the early 1990s, we inhabit a world that remains profoundly shaped by the struggles that brought into being so many of the member states that currently constitute the United Nations. One of the purposes of this brief book is to remind us that this past remains very much with us. It directs our attention both to the crises of empires and their continuities. It highlights the promises of nation-states and their limitations. And it insists on acknowledging the costs incurred by the transition from colonial subjugation to national independence, above all in terms of the millions of people who lost their lives and the millions more who were driven from their homelands. This, then, is not a celebratory account of decolonization; on the contrary, it attends to the problematic, even tragic, dimensions of this profoundly important series of events. So much of what decolonization realized—and failed to realize— remains relevant to the global challenges we face today.

Chapter 1
Waves of decolonization

Although decolonization is conventionally understood to refer to the political upheavals that brought an end to the European colonial empires and the establishment of nearly a hundred new nation-states across Africa, Asia, and the Pacific (the Third World) in the third quarter of the twentieth century, there were precedents for the events that the term "decolonization" was coined to characterize. Similar imperial crises had given rise to nearly two dozen nation-states in the American hemisphere (the New World) in the late eighteenth and early nineteenth centuries, and nearly a dozen more across central and eastern Europe (the Old World) in the early twentieth century. If these earlier upheavals are viewed through the lens of decolonization, they permit us to place the great transformation that brought into being the countries of the Third World in a wider historical context that enlarges our understanding of its causes and consequences.

New World decolonization

The first wave of decolonization occurred in the Americas. It started in 1776 with the rebellion by North American colonists against British rule, which led to the creation of the United States. This was followed in 1791 by the great slave revolt in the French colony of Saint-Domingue, a torturous struggle that eventuated in its independence as Haiti, the second country in the Western Hemisphere to break free of European control. By the early nineteenth century, wars of independence were sweeping across Spanish America, bringing into being a series of new nation-states that stretched from the plains of northern Mexico to the mountains of Patagonia. This period also brought an end to Portugal's control over Brazil, the largest of the South American territories.

The American Revolution was precipitated in large part because the global imperial struggle between Britain and France and their respective allies during the Seven Years' War (1756–63) placed intolerable economic and political strains on the relationship between the British imperial state and its North American colonists. When those colonists resorted to rebellion in 1776, their prospects for success were doubtful, but renewed war between Britain and its imperial rivals—starting with France in 1778, followed by Spain in 1779 and the Dutch Republic in 1780—helped turn the tide in the rebels' favor. At the same time, there was a risk that another empire would seek to control or even annex the rebellious colonies. One of the main aims of the Declaration of Independence was to assert America's status as a sovereign state, with "the full Power to levy War, conclude Peace, contract Alliances, establish Commerce, and to do all other Acts and Things which Independent States may of right do."

The rationale for this declaration was the radical idea of popular sovereignty, which presumed that political authority derived from "the People." This claim made the notion of the nation-state possible. But who were these people? The exodus of 60,000–100,000 loyalists after the war cleared some of the ideological space for a shared sense of national identity and political purpose among those who came to identify themselves as Americans, but its contours were crucially shaped as well by the denial of citizenship rights to indigenous Indians and enslaved Africans, as well as limitations on the rights of women. Insofar as the new state was

9

a nation, it was a nation delimited by race and gender. Moreover, it was a nation with imperial ambitions. As Thomas Jefferson famously declared, the United States was an "empire of liberty."

The subsequent New World revolts against imperial rule came about as a consequence of the French Revolutionary and Napoleonic wars (1792–1815), which were in important respects a continuation of the earlier global struggles between Britain and France. In the hugely profitable French sugar colony of Saint-Domingue, the slave revolt that broke out in 1791 might have met the fate of so many of its counterparts across the New World had it not been for the revolutionary upheaval in France. Not only did it inhibit efforts to restore imperial control, it also inspired many free blacks (and some whites) to join the revolt, giving it greater organizational and ideological direction. The revolutionaries in Paris sought to reconstitute the empire along liberal lines by abolishing slavery and granting citizenship rights to colonial subjects, but when Napoleon came to power, he reversed both actions, making independence the only feasible option for the island colony's rebels. An opportunistic attempt by the British to conquer Saint-Domingue ended in failure, as did Napoleon's subsequent bid to reclaim the colony. With the final destruction of the invading French forces in 1804, the colony became the country of Haiti. But the biggest beneficiary of this achievement may have been the United States, which purchased the Louisiana Territory from Napoleon after his plans to turn it into a granary for the Haitian plantation workforce he had hoped to re-enslave went awry. With this purchase, the United States doubled in size, the first great step in its march to continental domination.

For the Iberian colonies in the New World, the French invasions of Portugal and Spain in 1807–8 provided the main impetus of decolonization. The Portuguese royal court was able to flee to Brazil, but Napoleon lured Spain's king to Paris and deposed him. This created a power vacuum in Spanish America that many

1. Toussaint L'Ouverture, leader of the Haitian revolution, announces his new country's constitution on July 1, 1801. Rich in French revolutionary iconography, this propagandistic print also shows the Catholic Church endorsing Haitian independence, with God giving his benediction from on high.

colonists, especially creoles who claimed Spanish descent, sought to fill by asserting greater political autonomy. In 1812, Spain's government in exile in Cadiz drafted a liberal constitution that granted creoles—though not blacks or mulattos—representation in a newly created imperial parliament. British politicians like Edmund Burke had proposed a similar resolution to the American crisis, and the French would employ much the same strategy after World War II, when their new constitution granted citizenship rights to colonial peoples as part of an imperial Union. But opinion in Spanish America was divided over Cadiz, and, in any case, its political experiment came to an abrupt end with the restoration of the Spanish monarchy after Napoleon's fall. Efforts to reestablish royal authority in the Americas provoked intense and widespread resistance, eventually wearing down imperial forces. The restoration of the royal regime in Portugal provoked similar resistance in Brazil, though in this case the hostilities were less destructive and the outcome less revolutionary, with an independent Brazil retaining both monarchy and slavery.

Across Spanish America, the struggle against empire brought a multitude of new states into existence in the decade after the Napoleonic Wars, most of them issuing declarations of independence that echoed the American declaration. Like the authors of that document, they worried that other European empires might seek to annex them. They were aided in averting this outcome by the Monroe Doctrine (1823), which warned outside powers that the United States would oppose any interference in the affairs of the newly independent states in the American hemisphere, and by Britain's willingness to sign trade agreements that acknowledged the sovereignty of those states. Neither of these decisions was disinterested, however: both bespoke a determination to exert informal imperial influence over these fragile new countries, and in the British case it only came after earlier attempts to wield more direct power, including an abortive invasion of Argentina in 1806.

A distinguishing feature of the first wave of decolonization was the violence and disorder that accompanied it. There are no reliable casualty figures for any of these New World conflicts, but even piecemeal evidence indicates that they produced a terrible toll. As many as 100,000 combatants may have lost their lives in the American Revolution, either in combat or from malnutrition and disease, and this estimate does not include the huge losses from the smallpox epidemic that raged through the colonies during the conflict. Those who died during Saint-Domingue's protracted struggle for independence probably numbered in the hundreds of thousands. Moreover, successive waves of refugees fled from the conflict to other French colonies, Spanish America, and the United States (inadvertently introducing deadly yellow fever epidemics among their host populations). And the series of wars that culminated in independence for Spain's American colonies produced violence on a vast scale, leaving lasting scars on these societies. The royalist siege of Cartagena, for example, killed a third of the population of this large and important colonial city. The rebels were no less ruthless. The Argentine revolutionary Mariano Moreno advocated "cutting heads, spilling blood and sacrificing at all costs, even when it means adopting means that look like the customs of cannibals and Caribs."

An aggravating cause of this widespread violence was the absence of agreement among the rebels about the nature of the states they sought to create. The great revolutionary leader Simon Bolivar envisioned a Gran Columbia that encompassed the northern part of South America, but this ambitious endeavor collapsed amid civil war in 1830, leaving in its wake the countries of Venezuela, Colombia, and Ecuador. Similarly, advocates of a super-state in the southern portion of the continent could not overcome the centrifugal forces that resulted in the separate countries of Argentina, Uruguay, Paraguay, and Bolivia. Efforts to join Peru and Bolivia failed as well. A weak Central American Federation broke into five independent republics in 1839. Even those small republics had difficulty restraining the separatist ambitions of individual towns, which claimed municipal sovereignty. This fragmentation had nothing to do with any deeply rooted sense of nationalism among the inhabitants of those territories. Instead, it derived from the determination of landlords, merchants, and other local power brokers to retain their influence and protect their privileges. Their clash of interests undermined efforts to establish larger and more powerful composite states.

What happened in Latin America is perhaps less surprising than the United States' success in overcoming similar centrifugal forces. Under the Articles of Confederation that set the original terms of association among the thirteen colonies that claimed independence, the United States was designed to be a federation of autonomous sovereign states. The prospect that this constitutional arrangement would lead to political fragmentation were made evident as the separate states competed for western lands, imposed trade restrictions on one another, and threatened succession from the union. When resentment against agents of authority resulted in the armed uprising known as Shays' Rebellion in western Massachusetts in 1786, it became increasingly difficult to deny the need for a stronger central government. The following year's Constitutional Convention in Philadelphia drafted a new constitution that granted the federal government far greater power, providing it the means to collect tax revenues, maintain a military force, and oversee the incorporation of new territories within the United States. It laid the foundations for American expansion across the continent at the expense of Spain, France, Britain, Russia, and Mexico, not to mention a whole host of Indian polities.

Old World decolonization

Why was there a hundred-year time lag between this first wave of decolonization and the second? It certainly cannot be explained in terms of a golden era of contentment with colonial rule by subject peoples. The nineteenth and early twentieth centuries were marked by countless rebellions against empires. Many of those rebellions failed to articulate a vision of nationhood or statehood, but this was true of most successful New World rebellions in their early stages as well. Even the most significant upheavals, such as the Indian Mutiny/Rebellion of 1857, were usually crushed before they could create viable institutional and ideological infrastructures for state-building projects. This was due in part to the dramatic technological gulf that developed in this period between the military prowess of the major empires and the limited firepower available to most rebels. It was also a consequence of the fact that the period from 1815 to 1914 was free of the debilitating global wars that might have eroded imperial bonds and diminished empires' ability to suppress revolts.

Decolonization of a sort did occur across much of the Ottoman Empire's dominion in southeastern Europe, with peninsular Greece gaining independence in 1821, Serbia, Romania, and Bulgaria in 1878, and Albania in 1912. But rival empires played crucial roles in these upheavals, with the British and the French assisting the Greeks, the Russians supporting the new Slavic states and grabbing Ottoman lands for themselves, and the Hapsburgs annexing Bosnia-Herzegovina. Their contributions pointed to the real danger to enfeebled empires in this period—not decolonization but dismemberment by other powers. Japan announced its arrival on the international scene as an imperial power by wrenching Korea and Taiwan from China's control in 1895. And the United States made its bid for an overseas empire when it went to war against Spain in 1898, targeting that declining empire's remaining colonial possessions. For Cubans and Filipinos, whose struggles to overthrow Spanish rule had made significant strides, American intervention thwarted their efforts. Both territories, along with Guam and Puerto Rico, were ceded to the United States, which crushed the Philippine insurrection and hijacked Cuba's anticolonial struggle by turning the island into an informal protectorate.

What made the second wave of decolonization possible was World War I. In the estimation of the Russian revolutionary Vladimir Lenin, then observing the war from exile in Switzerland, this titanic struggle was, in his words, "an annexationist, predatory war of plunder" between imperial powers seeking "the partition and repartition" of the world. While there was much merit to this wartime assessment, it failed to anticipate the war's impact on the belligerent powers themselves, especially those that ruled central and eastern Europe. One Eurasian land empire after another crumbled under the strain of the war and its aftermath.

The first to fall was the Russian Empire in 1917. The collapse of the Czarist regime opened the door to the Bolsheviks, whose political survival necessitated that they sue for peace. Their surrender of Russia's western borderlands by terms of the German-dictated Brest-Litovsk treaty and the Germans' own subsequent defeat in November 1918 created the space for Poles, Finns, Estonians, and others to establish independent states. Georgians, Azerbaijanis, and other peoples made similar bids for freedom, but the Bolsheviks eventually overcame political fragmentation, civil war, and foreign intervention, reclaiming the Russian empire's southern and eastern provinces and recasting them on new ideological and organizational grounds as the Union of Soviet Socialist Republics.

No such reincarnation was available to the Hapsburg Empire. It dissolved with stunning speed at the end of the war, its imperial core reduced to the new rump state of Austria while the rest of the empire fragmented along ostensibly national lines, with Czechs, Poles, Hungarians, and others claiming sovereignty. The German Empire, the youngest and most aggressive of the continental European powers, was shorn of its overseas colonies and forced by the Versailles peace treaty to surrender substantial tracts of territory at home to neighboring states. Lastly, the war caused the 500-year-old Ottoman Empire to implode. Its sultanate was abolished, its Middle Eastern and European provinces lost, and its

Anatolian core reconstituted as the country of Turkey after a prolonged struggle.

It is worth noting that the only Eurasian land empire to escape a similar fate was China, arguably the weakest of these great states. Over the previous century a series of bloody peasant rebellions and the inexorable demands of foreign powers for concessions and unequal treaties had seriously eroded China's strength and autonomy. In 1911, the Qing dynasty collapsed and was succeeded by an ineffectual republican regime. Despite these difficulties, China passed through the war years largely unscathed. Although it declared war on Germany in 1917, it avoided any involvement in hostilities. As a result, its territorial boundaries remained largely intact. Most notably, it retained control of Tibet, Xinjiang, and Mongolia, lands where many indigenous inhabitants viewed the Chinese as imperial overlords.

While military defeat was the main precipitant of the political fragmentation of empires, even victory was no guarantee against the war's disintegrative effects. A prime example was the Irish war for independence, which resulted in the creation of the Irish Free State in 1922. This was a serious blow to British pride and power, and it offered a foretaste of the nationalist rebellions it would soon confront elsewhere in the empire. In many ways, however, Ireland was a special case—a territory physically separated from the imperial homeland by a narrow sea, settled by large numbers of Protestant colonists from England and Scotland but still populated predominantly by Catholic Irish, and nominally incorporated within the British political system, although a great many people had never fully reconciled themselves to this fact. Perhaps its closest counterpart was French Algeria, where similar problems would arise several decades later. Although militant nationalists failed to expel a war-distracted imperial government from Ireland in the Easter Rising of 1916, which was quickly crushed, they did lay the groundwork for the subsequent postwar struggle that produced an independent Irish state, albeit one shorn of the heavily Protestant-populated six counties of Northern Ireland.

What happened in Ireland in the aftermath of World War I is not normally characterized as decolonization, but for all practical purposes this was the outcome. Much the same can be said about the political changes that swept through central and eastern Europe after the war. From the ruins of empires arose the new countries of Czechoslovakia, Estonia, Finland, Hungary, Latvia, Lithuania, Poland, and Yugoslavia. None of them, it is true, were the products of prolonged struggles for independence. Indeed, most Czechs, Hungarians, and other peoples had remained acquiescent, even loyal, to the imperial regimes that ruled them during the war. But the fall of those regimes gave them an opportunity to envision new political futures by forging independent nation-states, and most did so with alacrity. Aiding their efforts was the peace settlement imposed by the victors, which instituted, in effect, decolonization from above. It justified the breakup of the defeated continental powers by embracing the principle of national self-determination, thereby conjoining idealism and *realpolitik* (a foreign policy informed by amoral self-interest). With the subsequent establishment of the League of Nations, this principle was enshrined as the new norm for international relations.

That norm, however, was qualified by a civilizational standard that the great powers deemed most non-European peoples unable to meet. Decolonization was thereby contained to the European continent. Elsewhere, the victors shared the imperial spoils of war. Germany's overseas colonies in Africa, Asia, and the Pacific were redistributed to Britain, France, Belgium, Japan, Australia, New Zealand, and South Africa. Britain and France divided the Ottoman Empire's Arab provinces between them, with the former claiming Iraq, Palestine, and Jordan while the latter got Syria and Lebanon. The prewar pretense of Ottoman suzerainty over Egypt was swept away, and the country became a formal British protectorate. Greece tried to create a "greater Greece" by annexing the western portion of Anatolia, which was heavily populated by Greeks. Only a revivified Turkish army under Mustafa Kemal (aka Atatürk) prevented this irredentist land-grab and forced the allies to accept an international treaty more favorable to Turkish national interests.

What the historian Erez Manela has termed "the Wilsonian moment"—that brief period immediately after the war when Woodrow Wilson's widely circulated statement promoting national self-determination inspired the mass mobilization of Egyptians, Indians, Vietnamese, and other colonial peoples in pursuit of that goal—was quickly replaced by disillusionment and anger when it became clear that the great powers intended to maintain the racial and geopolitical hierarchies that privileged the West over the rest. This was aptly illustrated by Wilson's veto of the racial equality clause that the Japanese had sought to include in the Paris peace agreement. Rebellions soon broke out against British and French authorities in Iraq, Syria, and Egypt. Indians under the leadership of Mohandas Gandhi launched their first mass civil disobedience campaign against the British Raj. The initial stirrings of anticolonial nationalism were felt in sub-Saharan Africa, with veterans of the Great War often leading the way. A million Koreans marched in the streets against their Japanese overlords. But the struggle against imperial rule was not conceived exclusively in terms of "national" liberation. Pan-African, pan-Arab, and pan-Asian ideas and organizations also gained strength in the years after the war, offering visions of a very differently constituted postcolonial world.

These challenges to colonial rule were largely suppressed or contained by the great powers during the interwar years. They made political concessions to indigenous elites in places like India and Egypt while elsewhere they refurbished the rhetoric of the white man's burden in the language of trusteeship and development. They created a system of mandates that draped the postwar grab for colonial territory in the benevolent guise of social and political advancement under the international oversight of the League of Nations (1920). They ensured that the decolonization of what would become known as the Third World would have to await another destabilizing clash of empires.

Meanwhile, postwar decolonization in the Old World proceeded in a fashion far more troubled than its proponents in Paris anticipated. Boundaries had to be drawn between the new states, provoking clashes over disputed territory between Russians and Poles, Poles and Czechs, Czechs and Hungarians, Hungarians and Austrians, Austrians and Yugoslavs, Yugoslavs and Italians, and more. Imbedded in the principle of national self-determination was the premise that nation-states would consist of homogeneous populations, but this proved all but impossible to achieve in most of the newly created states of central and eastern Europe. Scarcely half of Czechoslovakia's population was actually Czech. A third of Poland's population consisted of Ukrainians, Belarussians, Lithuanians, and other non-Poles. Five million Germans found themselves living within the newly drawn borders of Poland and Czechoslovakia. Three million Hungarians lived outside Hungary's borders. A potpourri of Croats, Muslims, Macedonians, Serbs, and Slovenes comprised the cobbled together country of Yugoslavia. And scattered across the region were millions of Jews, most of them marginalized within these new nation-states.

The Paris peace agreement (1919) required all of these newly established countries to sign treaties promising to protect the rights of minorities within their borders, but the requirement proved impossible to enforce. The persecution of minorities, especially Jews, became widespread. Perhaps as many as ten million refugees fled their homes in the years immediately after the war. The problem of population transfers—along with the ethnic cleansing that often accompanied it—was especially apparent in territories previously ruled by the Ottoman Empire. Here the Ottoman government's wartime efforts to expel or

2. Turkish troops enter Smyrna (now Izmir) on September 9, 1922. Some 300,000 Greek and Armenian refugees clogged Smyrna's docks, seeking escape from the approaching Turks. Over the next four days, much of Smyrna burned and tens of thousands of refugees died. This notorious event highlighted the ethnic violence that often accompanied nation-building after World War I.

exterminate the Armenian population had resulted in 800,000 deaths and a global diaspora of survivors. The postwar clash between Turkey and Greece produced terrible massacres of civilians—perhaps as many as 100,000 in Smyrna (Izmir) alone—and the deportation of nearly a million Greeks from Anatolia and 400,000 Muslims from Macedonia.

In Ireland, the British attempted to avoid civil war between Catholics and Protestants by pressing for partition. The Anglo-Irish Treaty of 1921 stipulated that the six counties of Northern Ireland, with its large pool of Protestants, would remain within the United Kingdom. The Irish negotiators who agreed to this concession set off a year-long civil war between the nationalists' pro- and antitreaty factions. And the treaty itself failed to prevent sectarian clashes on both sides of the new border. In the south, Protestant landlords were driven off their estates and their country houses were burned to the ground. In the north, Protestants launched what has been described as a pogrom against Catholic communities. Nowhere were its effects more devastating than in the city of Belfast, where 650 houses and businesses were destroyed, 8,000 residents fled their homes, and nearly 500 individuals—two-thirds of them Catholics—were killed.

Although ethnic and religious conflicts within the new nation-states of the Old World soon died down, as did the border disputes between those states, they did not disappear. Antagonisms and resentments festered in the interwar years, fueling extremist movements across the Continent. The Nazi regime that came to power in 1933 fed on such grievances, fostering hatred of Jews as aliens undermining the nation, bitterness about Germany's territorial diminishment under the terms of the Versailles peace settlement, and outrage at Czechoslovakia and Poland's treatment of their German minorities. Across central and eastern Europe, Jews were persecuted by anti-Semitic governments. The Soviets, meanwhile, conducted massive population transfers and ruthless campaigns of expropriation and starvation against targeted groups in Belarus, Ukraine, and neighboring territories. Another devastating war would be required to give greater ethnic homogeneity and territorial fixity to the nation-states of Europe—a war that produced unprecedented campaigns of ethnic cleansing and population transfer, including the extermination of six million Jews and the expulsion of 12 to 14 million Germans from eastern Europe.

Preludes to Third World decolonization

The two waves of decolonization that preceded the decolonization of the Third World reveal several recurring themes. One is the importance of global wars between empires as catalysts of decolonization. Not only did these wars open the door to successive waves of decolonization; they also made violence an integral element of the process of transition. A further source of conflict arose as a result of contending conceptions of what that transition was intended to achieve. Although the nation-state became the leading option, it was hardly the only one, and its composition and constituency were in any case far from self-evident. The struggle to determine the new states' territorial dimensions, ethnic composition, and other defining characteristics frequently led to civil war, ethnic cleansing, and refugee populations. In the end, though, these waves of decolonization did not drive empires into extinction. Empires were resolute and resourceful, and they often managed to reconstitute themselves in new forms. The larger meaning to be drawn from these themes is that decolonization has a longer and more complex history that requires a more nuanced and less celebratory—not to mention less exceptionalist—analysis than it often receives.

Decolonization did not simply recur in some cyclical pattern, however; it began at a particular place and point in time, and each subsequent wave built on the one that preceded it. While a few colonies may remain today, they exist as outliers in an international order that endorses the principle of popular sovereignty and the norm of nation-states. This is a very different world from the one that prevailed when the first wave of decolonization crashed through the protective levees of empires. However much subject peoples might have resented being ruled by imperial autocrats, they rarely were able to escape their subjugation, and those that did often faced the choice of subjugating other peoples or themselves being resubjugated by some other empire. The wave of decolonization that swept through the New World from the late eighteenth through the early nineteenth century offered another possibility: the establishment of nation-states that ostensibly offered their populations the right of self-determination. However problematic its execution, this seductive and subversive idea took a powerful hold on the political imaginations of peoples around the world.

The shattering effects of World War I on the belligerent powers, especially the Eurasian land empires, gave many of their subjects a previously unimagined opportunity to claim national independence. Even those subjects who had been relatively content with their place and status within empires were propelled by the postwar power vacuum to forge nation-states of their own. With the establishment of the League of Nations, the nation-state and the new notion of sovereignty it embodied had become increasingly integral to the international order. Even the victorious powers, which took the opportunity to acquire new colonial possessions after the war, characterized themselves as nation-states as well as empires. In order to support this claim, however, they had to draw an increasingly stark distinction between their metropolitan cores, where popular sovereignty applied, and their colonial peripheries, where it did not. The latter territories were understood to be part of the state, but not the nation. Moreover, their indigenous populations were disqualified from claiming self-determination on self-serving "civilizational" grounds. The European colonial empires found it increasingly difficult to defend this position, especially in the aftermath of World War II. Though it was possible for empires to survive this upheaval, it gradually became clear that colonialism itself could not.

Chapter 2
Global war's colonial consequences

If there is some merit to Lenin's charge that World War I was caused by empires seeking to redivide the world, such an assessment makes even more sense for World War II. The imperial ambitions of Germany and Japan precipitated the conflict. These expansionist powers confronted a world divided into two distinct kinds of polities: nation-states that insisted on the inviolability of their sovereignty and colonial empires that imposed their authority on nearly everyone else. German and Japanese empire-building could occur only by subverting the sovereignty of the former and supplanting the authority of the latter.

The Second World War's impact on the international order was even more transformative than that of the First. It produced disorder and destruction on an unprecedented scale, destabilizing states and societies across much of the world. While Germany and Japan failed in their bids to build vast new empires that endured, the established European colonial empires (especially Britain, France, and the Netherlands) found their own imperial authority fatally weakened as well. The war simultaneously eroded the foundations of colonial rule as a form of governance, which increasingly came under challenge from independence movements across Asia and Africa, and laid the groundwork for alternative modes of imperial power, made manifest by the global rivalry between the United

States and the Soviet Union. The European empires fought fiercely to retain their colonial possessions after the war, and they gained some advantage from the onset of the Cold War. In the end, however, they were unable to prevent decolonization from spreading from one region to another, producing a multitude of new nation-states in what would soon be characterized as the Third World.

Imperial war

While historians continue to debate the full extent of Hitler's imperial ambitions, they agree that those ambitions focused first and foremost on the acquisition of *lebensraum* (living space) in the region east of Germany, which Timothy Snyder has aptly termed the "bloodlands." Hitler sought, in effect, to reverse the decolonization of the Old World by annexing territory in central and eastern Europe, exterminating or enslaving its indigenous populations, and colonizing the land with German peoples. (Hitler was initially aided and abetted by Stalin, who wanted to recover the eastern European territories Russia had lost at Brest-Litovsk.) The fragility of the new nation-states forged in the aftermath of the First World War made them tempting targets for conquest by Nazi Germany, much as their New World predecessors had been for European empires in the late eighteenth and early nineteenth centuries.

Hitler's bid to establish an empire that stretched across Europe echoed the earlier ambitions of Napoleon. Unlike his predecessor, however, Hitler sought to institute racial hierarchies and slave labor within Europe itself. In this regard there is a good deal of truth to the claim that Hitler applied to the European arena the same ruthless principles and policies that Europeans had long practiced against the peoples they subjugated overseas. The Third Reich managed during its relatively brief reign to systematically exterminate six million Jews, along with large numbers of Slavs and others it classified as inferior races.

The Nazis encouraged Germans to settle in the bloodlands, where ethnic cleansing had swept away many of the prior inhabitants. But the colonizing ambitions of the Nazi state came to naught as the Soviet army advanced westward. Millions of German civilians fled from Czechoslovakia, Hungary, Poland, and neighboring countries in the face of the enemy's advance, and millions more were expelled in the war's immediate aftermath. The postwar political order uprooted other ethnic groups as well: 1.5 million ethnic Poles were deported from what was then deemed Soviet territory to Poland, while half a million ethnic Ukrainians were forced from Poland to Soviet Ukraine. Population transfers also affected Slovaks, Magyars, Serbs, Croats, and others. Ironically, Hitler's most enduring legacy across the region may have been the restoration of the very nation-states he had sought to destroy, reconstituted as more ethnically homogeneous entities as a result of the mass exterminations and forced migrations the war had precipitated.

Imperial Japan's simultaneous bid to redraw the map of Asia was similarly organized around racial subordination, forced labor, and population transfers. While dressing itself in the pan-Asianist garb of the Greater East Asian Co-Prosperity Sphere, Japan quickly disabused many of its neighbors of any expectations that they would become equal partners in an ethnic alliance to escape European colonial oppression. Instead, Japanese authorities treated them as inferior races to be subjugated and exploited. Like Germany, Japan also sought living space for its surplus population. Millions of Japanese had already settled in Korea, Taiwan, and Manchuria (renamed Manchukuo), and many more would occupy the territories acquired by Japan after 1941. Defeat in 1945 made these Japanese colonists' positions untenable. This was especially the case in Manchuria, where the Soviet advance caused the precipitate flight of more than a million settlers, mirroring the plight of their German counterparts in eastern Europe. By the end of 1946, some five million Japanese had been repatriated to their island homeland, now entirely divested of its empire.

Italy, the third main member of the Axis alliance, had sought to extend its imperial reach during the war as well. It pushed into the eastern Mediterranean and envisioned an expansion of its empire in North and East Africa at the expense of the British. But it met the same fate as its Axis allies. With the fall of the fascist regime, Italy was shorn of its colonies. Some 350,000 Italian colonists were repatriated to their motherland from Libya, Eritrea, Ethiopia, Somaliland, and Balkan territories during and after the war.

The havoc wrought by World War II on subject populations across the colonial world has only recently attracted serious scholarly attention. It destroyed trade networks and disrupted economies, precipitated deadly epidemics and famines, gave rise to the widespread use of forced labor, and drove great numbers of people from their homes. Among the most deadly disasters were the famines that swept across Asia as a result of disruptions in trade and transport and the deliberate diversion of resources by the belligerent powers. In Vietnam, the appropriation of rice supplies by the Japanese for their own needs precipitated a famine that killed as many as two million people in 1944–45. Similar policies produced a similar outcome across Indonesia, where an estimated 2.4 million Javanese and other Indonesians starved to death. Millions more fell victim to famine in war-torn China, especially in Henan province in 1943–44. Perhaps the most devastating famine was the one that struck the Indian province of Bengal. The Japanese occupation of Burma and Thailand cut off essential rice imports to the province, and food shortages were further exacerbated by the scorched earth tactics British forces used to slow the Japanese advance and the destructive cyclone that swept through the region in late 1942. Even as the scale of the disaster became apparent in 1943, wheat and rice continued to be exported from other parts of India; Winston Churchill, Britain's prime minister, adamantly opposed any government assistance to the famine victims. In the end, some three to four million Bengalis are believed to have died.

The use of coerced labor was widespread across Asia during the war, with the belligerent powers mobilizing colonial subjects to lay out roads and rail lines, build bridges and ports, load and unload ships and planes, and more. The British, for example, put nearly 200,000 Naga tribesmen to work as porters, carrying military supplies through the densely forested highlands of Southeast Asia. The Japanese were especially ruthless in their use of forced labor. One of the most infamous instances was the so-called death railway they built from Bangkok to Rangoon, which cost the lives of half the 180,000 civilians and a fifth of the 60,000 prisoners of war who were forced to construct it. The Japanese also shipped off close to a quarter million Javanese peasants to work on war-related projects across the Indonesian archipelago: most of them never returned home alive.

Wartime upheaval and deprivation afflicted people in other parts of the colonial world as well. Many North Africans were displaced by the armies that swept across the region, and they experienced food shortages that led to localized famines. Sub-Saharan Africans, although largely untouched by combat, endured trade disruptions and resource demands that generated crises in certain communities. A famine in Ruanda-Urundi produced an estimated 300,000 victims (probably a higher per capita death toll than the Bengal famine). African colonial regimes ratcheted up the production of raw materials and the exploitation of local labor to aid the imperial war effort. While foreign companies and white settlers generally profited from the heightened demand for minerals, fibers, and other raw materials, Africans rarely did. Some 100,000 Nigerians were forced to work in that colony's tin mines. Nearly the same number of Tanzanians was rounded up to service the sisal and rubber plantations. More generally, wartime controls on colonial economies reduced wages, increased prices, and placed other burdens on subject peoples.

Disruptive in a different way was the mobilization of colonial subjects for military service. When Free French forces supplanted

3. Ashanti troops from the British West African colony of the Gold Coast rest during a march in 1942. They were just a few of the millions of colonial subjects who were mobilized by the imperial powers for service as soldiers and laborers during World War II. Many were politicized by the experience and became active in postwar anticolonial campaigns.

the Vichy regime in North Africa in 1942, they recruited some 250,000 North Africans to join in the subsequent invasions of Italy and France. Many of them were changed men when they returned, impatient for economic opportunities and political rights. Nearly half a million of Britain's African subjects contributed to the war effort, serving as combatants and auxiliary personnel in Burma, Egypt, and other theaters of war. New horizons and new ideas transformed many of them, including Hussein Onyango Obama, President Barack Obama's paternal grandfather, a Luo from Kenya who served as an army cook in

Burma; he later fell afoul of colonial authorities for his political activity. The Indian army grew from 200,000 to 2.5 million men between 1939 and 1945, an unprecedented expansion of military manpower that would leave the British more susceptible to pressure for independence as those forces became less tractable and trustworthy toward the end of the war.

Across the colonial world, the cumulative effects of the war created more restive and resentful populations that possessed greater will and capacity than ever before to challenge their subjugation. This was especially evident in India, where the struggle against British rule had already made major strides in the interwar years. The war brought the conflict between the British and their Indian opponents to a head. When the viceroy in September 1939 declared India's entry into the war without consulting Indian leaders, Mohandas Gandhi and his Indian National Congress colleagues protested by ceasing all cooperation with British authorities. Stafford Cripps, a member of the British war cabinet, was dispatched to India in 1942 to work out a deal: he promised that India would gain self-government soon after the war. Negotiations broke down over the time frame and the meaning of independence, and Congress leaders soon launched the "Quit India" campaign.

The insurrection that followed became the most serious challenge to British imperial authority since the Indian Mutiny/Rebellion of 1857. Telegraph and rail lines were cut across the country and more than two hundred police stations were burned down during the uprising. It became obvious to all parties that Britain's days as India's overlord were numbered. The key question was what sort of political order would come into existence when the British left. Churchill favored the balkanization of India into "Pakistan, Hindustan, and Princestan," all of them sufficiently weak and suspicious of the others to ensure continued imperial control of the region. The Labour government, which took office in July 1945, was equally intent on maintaining influence in the subcontinent, but it envisioned some sort of federated polity that would safeguard the interests of Muslims and other minorities and become a member of the British Commonwealth so as to ensure that India's vast reserves of manpower could continue to be tapped for military use elsewhere in the empire. Congress wanted a strong, nonsectarian, resolutely nonaligned state that would incorporate all of the territory that comprised British India. The Muslim League gravitated toward an increasingly intransigent insistence on a separate state for Muslims. Hyderabad, Mysore, and other large princely states proclaimed their sovereignty and opposed incorporation into any successor to the Raj. These differences would only loom larger as the prospects for independence grew closer.

For the vast swathe of territory that extended east of India, invasion and occupation by Japanese forces was the main impetus for imperial destabilization. Ever since its surprise victory in the Russo-Japanese War of 1904-5, Japan had been a source of inspiration for anticolonial activists across Asia, providing an example and a refuge for many of them. Although Japan's increasingly belligerent behavior in the interwar years disillusioned some Asian critics of colonialism, others remained convinced that its military might and slogan of "Asia for the Asians" offered the best avenue of escape from colonial subjugation. The Japanese forces that swept through Southeast Asia with such astonishing speed in 1941-42 presented themselves as the region's liberators from Western colonialism, and they were welcomed as such by many locals. Nationalist leaders from Burma to Indonesia to the Philippines collaborated with the Japanese, who reciprocated by granting them some degree of self-government over time. The Indonesian nationalist Sukarno and his associates forged a mutually beneficial association with the occupying authorities. So did some prominent Filipinos. The Burmese nationalist Aung San worked closely with the Japanese until 1944, when he realized that the tide of war was turning and opportunistically switched sides. Even a leading Indian nationalist, Subhas Chandra Bose, looked to Japan to liberate his country. He traveled to Tokyo and recruited more than a 100,000 Indian prisoners of war for the Indian National Army, which was created to aid the Japanese in driving the British from India. Dato Onn bin Ja'afar, one of the early leaders of independent Malaya, spoke for many of his Southeast Asian contemporaries when he noted: "Under the Japanese I learnt that an Asian is just as good as a European.... [The Japanese] were brutal, true, but they inspired us with a new idea of what Asia might become."

While some anticolonial nationalists collaborated with the Japanese, others resisted them. In French Indochina, where Vichy authorities welcomed the Japanese as their ally and continued to govern the region until late in the war, the Viet Minh fought to expel these new occupiers. For the Vietnamese nationalist Ho Chi Minh, the Japanese had shown their true imperialist colors by bolstering Vichy French rule. Japan's brutal war against China turned Malaya's large ethnic Chinese population against the Japanese invaders as well. The Malayan People's Anti-Japanese Army, which spearheaded the struggle against them, drew mainly from the Chinese community; the British rewarded its leader, Chin Peng, with the Order of the British Empire, an honor rich in irony in light of his subsequent struggle to expel the British from Malaya. In Burma, Karen and other tribal peoples in the highlands steadfastly opposed the Japanese and harassed their supply lines. In each of these cases, the campaigns to drive out the Japanese would carry over into resistance to the postwar regimes, which meant reconstituted colonial regimes in the Malayan and Vietnamese cases.

The maelstrom of war made itself felt across the entire colonial world, though most acutely in Asia. Here it forced anticolonial activists to choose sides in the titanic struggle between empires, a decision that carried considerable personal and political risk. At the same time, it provided an unprecedented opportunity for these activists to leverage the crisis to their advantage, using it to advance the aim of independence. It soon became apparent, however, that this could not be done in most cases without a fight.

The postwar ambitions of the colonial empires

When World War II came to a close—in May 1945 in Europe and August 1945 in Asia—the great colonial empires lay in ruins. The destruction was complete in the case of the Axis powers: Japan and Italy lost all their prewar colonial possessions as well as their war gains, while Germany was not only stripped of the territories it had acquired from the annexation of Austria onward, but its homeland was divided into separate zones, with the eastern zone subject to Soviet domination. France, the Netherlands, and Belgium had found themselves in much the same position during the war as the non-Western colonies they controlled—the victims of imperial conquest. Their own subjugation did not instill greater empathy for or insight into the plight of the peoples they had subjugated, but it did erode the ideological and political foundations of their empires. Japan's stunning success across Asia and the Pacific had a corresponding effect on the British, French, Dutch, and American colonies that fell to its armies: the fleeing colonizers would never again command the authority they had exerted over their colonial subjects before the war. Even in India, which remained in British hands, the war marked a critical turning point. Only in sub-Saharan Africa, the Caribbean, and a few other regions—mainly those places that had escaped the direct impact of war—did colonial rule still seem secure. Yet even there subtle forces were at work that would destabilize colonial authority.

The major colonial empires, however, refused to accept their demise as a fait accompli. On the contrary, they looked to recover their colonial possessions, seeking to renew and in some respects reinvent their imperial missions. In the midst of World War II, the Dutch government-in-exile in London announced plans to create a postwar commonwealth that would preserve the empire and supply the economic resources needed to rebuild the Netherlands, though it cast itself in the role of liberator of the Indonesians from Japanese oppressors. France's collaborationist Vichy regime devoted considerable attention to the economic development—more often than not a euphemism for economic exploitation—of its colonies, and many of these policies persisted when Free French forces took over. General Charles de Gaulle saw the renewal of the French empire after the war as essential to France's recovery as a great power. At a conference in Brazzaville in French Equatorial Africa in 1944, he promised colonial peoples more voice in their own affairs, but only by means of closer political integration with France. "The goals of the task of civilization, accomplished by France in her colonies," declared the preamble to the conference recommendations, "rule out any idea of autonomy, any possibility of evolution outside the French block of empire. The eventual creation, even in the distant future, of self-government in the colonies is to be set aside."

When that unabashed imperialist Winston Churchill declared in Parliament in 1942 that he had not become prime minister "in order to preside over the liquidation of the British Empire," he was voicing a view widely shared by his contemporaries. Not only did the British hope to recover the colonies they had lost during the war, they actually envisioned enlarging their empire. From their perch in India's summer capital of Simla, Burma's exiled colonial official made plans both for the reoccupation of Burma *and* the occupation of Thailand. Britain's imperial ambitions in Asia were so blatant during the war that American officials sarcastically suggested that the acronym SEAC (South East Asia Command) actually meant Save England's Asian Colonies. The Middle East and the Mediterranean basin offered opportunities for imperial expansion as well. The British responded to Axis threats in the region by imposing puppet regimes on Egypt, Iraq, and Iran. The latter country was divided into two spheres of influence, with the north under Soviet control while the oil-rich south became the bailiwick of the British, and they were determined to retain it.

4. General Charles de Gaulle, leader of the Free French forces during World War II, gives the opening speech at the Brazzaville Conference in French Equatorial Africa in 1944. He promised to transform the relationship between France and its colonies, though the declaration that concluded the conference categorically rejected political independence for colonial territories.

Some imperial officials envisioned Greece as a colony, convinced that the Greeks were incapable of governing themselves. Others wanted to acquire Cyrenaica (the eastern portion of Libya) as a strategic buffer for Egypt and the Suez Canal. Italy's colonies as a whole looked like easy pickings for a resurgent empire.

Britain's expansionist ambitions proved to be a pipe dream, and even its plans to maintain its existing empire and reclaim the territories lost in the war were fraught with peril. Not only were ex-colonial subjects less amenable to the restoration of the prewar status quo ante than the British anticipated. So too were their wartime allies, the United States and the Soviet Union, each of whom had reasons of its own—both ideological and geopolitical—to oppose a revivified British Empire. Moreover, Britain was scarcely able to feed and house its own population at the end of the war, much less expand or even maintain an empire abroad. Its cities were in ruins, its trade networks shattered, its economy mired in debt. As John Maynard Keynes, the great economist and advisor to the government, pointed out, "We cannot police half the world at our own expense when we have already gone into pawn on the other half."

Yet the country's postwar economic plight also helps explain its leaders' determination to restore and revitalize the empire. The territories it had lost during the war to Japan were treasure troves of resources. They included oil from Borneo, timber from Burma, and, above all, tin and rubber from Malaya. The petroleum reserves of the Middle East, especially the oil fields of Iran and Iraq, assumed increased importance as well. The wartime boom in the exploitation of sub-Saharan Africa's agricultural and mineral resources persuaded British officials that the region could be developed into a new India, the economic engine of an imperial resurgence.

What followed has been called the "second colonial occupation" of Africa, Southeast Asia, and other dependent territories. Colonial officials, aided by an army of technical experts, scrambled to exploit mineral resources, improve agricultural yields, and promote development projects. At a time when the British public remained under a strict system of food rationing, the government committed economic resources to the empire through the Colonial Development and Welfare Act of 1945. The act provided £12 million per annum to the economic and social development of the colonies. (The funds were drawn not from British taxpayers but from wartime reserves the colonies had accumulated in London.) Some of these development projects were notorious failures. The most notable example was the Tanganyika groundnut scheme, which wasted millions of pounds in a misbegotten effort to get African peasants to grow peanuts to meet the acute shortage of edible oils in postwar Britain. Other projects, however, succeeded spectacularly: the funds invested in Malaya's tin and rubber industries brought handsome benefits to the British economy. Undergirding the entire postwar strategy to link economic recovery to imperial development was the Sterling Area, a closed currency zone that funneled colonial trade through Britain, kept colonies' sterling balances under metropolitan control, and restricted foreign access to colonial markets and resources.

In 1946 the French government established a similar scheme for its colonies, the Economic and Social Development Fund, and the Dutch, Belgian, and Portuguese governments all asserted their intention to invest in the development of their colonies as well. One purpose of these programs and pronouncements was to counter critic of colonialism, gaining traction in the international arena by casting colonial initiatives as the counterparts of domestic social welfare schemes intended to assist primitive peoples in their march to modernity. Yet none of the imperial powers made any serious investments in health, education, and other welfare programs for their colonial subjects. Instead, they channeled funds into commodity production schemes, land conservation programs, infrastructural construction projects, and various other economic initiatives designed to aid in the economic recovery of the imperial metropole. They also equated national prestige and patriotism with the revival of their imperial missions. Charles de Gaulle, for example, was determined to restore French pride, which had been shattered by its defeat and occupation by Germany, and his strategy for doing so hinged on a resurgent French empire. Postwar angst among Dutch, Belgian, and Portuguese officials was accentuated by their countries' diminutive size, which caused them to conclude that the loss of their overseas possessions would consign them to insignificance in the postwar world. They sought desperately to prevent this outcome by clinging to their colonies.

Empires on the ropes

While Britain and its counterparts were certainly resourceful in responding to the challenges that the postwar era posed for colonial empires, they confronted unprecedented pressures from colonial peoples seeking independence. Across large parts of South and Southeast Asia, those pressures proved impossible to contain. Nowhere did the collapse of imperial rule occur more quickly or completely in the immediate aftermath of the war than it did in the "Crown Jewel" of the British Empire, India. The stunning Indian naval mutiny of 1946, the rapid escalation of communal violence between Hindus and Muslims, and the corresponding breakdown of the political authority of the Raj combined to undermine the Labour government's plans for India to remain in the imperial orbit as a single, self-governing Dominion. With unseemly haste, the British pushed up the date of independence from 1948 to 1947, acceded to the Muslim League's demand for partition, and scuttled from the subcontinent, leaving it divided into two hostile states. Their only consolation was that both India and Pakistan agreed to become members of the Commonwealth, but only after the British retreated from the requirement that the monarchy be recognized as the organization's symbolic head.

The British departure from Burma was no less ignominious. All hopes that they would be able to restore the prewar colonial order were shattered by Aung San and his battle-hardened Burma National Army. No longer able to call on Indian forces to crush nationalist resistance, the British were obliged to grant Burma its independence in January 1948. And Burma's new rulers did not even grant them the consoling gesture of agreeing to entry into the Commonwealth.

A counterpoint to the collapse of the Raj in India/Pakistan and Burma was the transfer of power in Ceylon, where in 1948 the British got everything they had failed to gain in the other cases. The Sinhalese who negotiated Ceylon's independence welcomed continued ties to their former master's defense and foreign policy, and embraced admission into the Commonwealth. They accepted this neocolonial relationship as a necessary counterweight to their Indian neighbor to the north, a nascent geopolitical behemoth whose regional interests and ambitions worried them. Similar concerns would allow the British to forge equivalent relationships with various other ex-colonies in the future.

The British had more success in restoring control over the other colonies they lost to the Japanese during the war, notably Malaya, Borneo, Singapore, and Hong Kong. They also dispatched troops to Indochina and the Indonesian archipelago, laying the groundwork for the reestablishment of French and Dutch control of these territories. In both cases, however, long-standing nationalist movements had already proclaimed their countries' independence. Not surprisingly, the allies' actions ran into resistance from locals, whose deference to any form of imperial authority had largely been shattered by the war. Long pent-up resentments against the colonizers broke to the surface with deadly attacks on Europeans freed from Japanese internment camps. Some 200 Dutch ex-internees were slaughtered by mobs in Surabaya, Indonesia's second largest city. British military occupation of Surabaya exacerbated the crisis. Clashes between Indonesians and the British escalated into one of the most intense battles of the immediate postwar era, causing 15,000 Indonesian and 600 British casualties and leaving the city in utter ruin. This proved to be the opening skirmish in the Indonesian war for independence.

In Vietnam, Ho Chi Minh's Viet Minh had declared independence only days after the surrender of Japan, but Chinese and British forces quickly occupied the country, paving the way for the restoration of French rule. Angry Vietnamese responded by massacring more than a hundred French civilians in Saigon. French forces, assisted by rearmed Japanese prisoners, drove the Viet Minh from Hanoi and other cities, killing as many as 6,000 Vietnamese in the port city of Haiphong alone. Here again the anticolonial struggle for independence had begun in earnest.

Given the widespread devastation and lasting trauma that the war had inflicted on the peoples of Asia, it is not surprising that political instability and violence persisted across the region long after the official cessation of hostilities. Social order had been shattered, leaving communities distrustful of one another and susceptible to savagery. Recent research has shown, for example, that the postwar turmoil in Vietnam ranged well beyond the struggle between the French and the Viet Minh: it involved ruthless efforts to liquidate competing political parties and bloody clashes between different ethnic and religious groups. Nor was this systemic violence limited to the regions where Europeans were reinstituting colonial rule. In Korea, American occupying forces suppressed a peasant uprising in 1946, precipitated by a poor harvest and reports that the great powers intended to place their country in trusteeship for five years. This was followed by a popular insurgency on the island of Cheju that US-assisted Korean militias put down with extreme ferocity, killing some 30,000 to 60,000 insurgents. And none of the postwar conflicts in Asia were more deadly and destructive than the civil war between Nationalist and Communist forces in China, which produced a casualty count in the millions. Europeans, then, could chalk up some of the challenges they confronted in the east to the lingering instability left by World War II.

Yet there were troubling developments in less traumatized parts of the colonial world as well. In Madagascar, the large island off the southeast coast of Africa that had largely escaped the storms of war, a major rebellion broke out against French colonial rule in 1947. It was suppressed with extraordinary ferocity, with the official death toll put at 80,000, though it was almost certainly much higher. The French also encountered troubles in Algeria, where a public rally celebrating the end of the war in Europe led to a clash with police in the town of Sétif, which escalated into regional unrest and a military crackdown. At least 1,500 people, mostly Muslims, were killed, though some nationalists placed the figure as high as 45,000, and the incident bode ill for Algeria's future.

The Accra riots that broke out in 1948 were small beer by the standards of Madagascar or Algeria, but they sent shock waves to the Colonial Office, which regarded the Gold Coast as one of Britain's most prosperous and contented colonies in Africa. The trouble began when police fired on a group of African ex-servicemen marching on the governor's residence to protest unemployment and unpaid war pensions. Five days of rioting followed, leaving 29 dead and 237 wounded. The modern nationalist movement that would win independence for the newly renamed nation of Ghana nine years later had been set in motion.

And then there was the Middle East, where both the French and the British discovered that the war had seriously eroded the foundations of their imperial authority. Lebanese and Syrian nationalists had declared their independence from France in late 1943, but the French refused to recognize those claims and sent troops—mainly North and West African regiments—to reassert authority in May 1945. Damascus was shelled, and hundreds of Syrians were killed and buried in unmarked graves. The British Middle East Command soon intervened, bringing the French action—and its ambitions in Syria and Lebanon—to an abrupt and ignominious end.

For the British, Palestine proved the most troubled and tragic imperial crisis they faced outside the Asian sphere in the immediate postwar years. A situation that had seemed intractable enough before the outbreak of World War II became even more so after 1945; the British found it increasingly impossible not only to reconcile the competing interests and ambitions of Arabs and Jews but to maintain their own self-proclaimed position as neutral mediators. The actions of Zionist terrorists—especially the bombing of the King David Hotel, headquarters of the British government in Jerusalem, attempts to assassinate foreign secretary Ernest Bevin and other British officials, and the notorious hanging of two kidnapped British soldiers, whose bodies were then booby-trapped to inflict further casualties—stirred anti-Semitic sentiments among the British and sparked unprovoked attacks on Jewish civilians by security forces. By 1947, Britain had stationed 100,000 troops (a tenth of its entire army) in Palestine, amounting to one soldier for every eighteen residents of the mandated territory. But this overwhelming military presence simply accelerated the cycle of violence, causing the situation to spiral out of Britain's control. With its actions alienating allies on both sides of the conflict—friendly Arab states, which were sympathetic to the Palestinian cause, and the United States, which favored the creation of a Jewish state—Britain simply surrendered its mandate to the United Nations in 1948 and withdrew from Palestine as Jews and Arabs prepared for war.

Each of these crises was unique, the product of particular causes and contexts. Taken together, however, they reveal that the European colonial empires in the immediate aftermath of World War II confronted a common set of challenges. The war had seriously weakened their authority over colonial subjects, especially in Asia, but elsewhere as well. A strategic retreat from some overseas possessions proved inescapable. Yet the political and economic challenges that these empires confronted after the war compelled them to retain, recover, and reassert their imperial authority wherever they could do so.

New imperial formations

While the traditional European imperial powers were seeking to revitalize or at least hold on to their colonial territories, the postwar international environment was making such empires increasingly outmoded. This transformation is often interpreted as a rejection of imperialism tout court, but it might be more accurately understood as a shift to new imperial formations that were less incompatible with nationalism.

The rise of the United States and the Soviet Union as postwar superpowers pointed the way to these new imperial formations.

Both of these states had a range of reasons—ideological, political, and economic—to regard European efforts to rebuild their prewar colonial orders with disfavor. True, the United States would substantially soften its stance toward European allies' imperial holding actions as the Cold War made it more fearful that colonial subjects clamoring for freedom were merely acting as dupes of a worldwide communist conspiracy. But the more profound postwar development was that both the United States and its rival for global supremacy were forging empires that did not rely on colonial rule, and hence were more compatible with an international order that increasingly considered the nation-state its universal baseline.

From its founding in 1923, the Soviet Union had sought to accommodate nationalist sentiments within its new model empire by depoliticizing those sentiments and absorbing them in its federated constitutional structure. After 1945, it was able to recover territories it had lost during the war and expand its territorial boundaries both in the west and the east. But the most significant expression of its postwar empire-building was the chain of client states it created across eastern Europe. Genuinely independent voices in these states were soon silenced and governments installed that became puppets of Soviet interests. Yet these states claimed national sovereignty and gained membership in the United Nations.

The United States forged its own new model empire after the war. In 1946 the United States fulfilled its prewar pledge to grant independence to the Philippines, an action that stood in stark contrast to the contemporaneous conduct of European colonial powers. Yet what seemed to be the renunciation of empire assumed a rather different character on closer analysis. In return for ceding sovereignty over the Philippines, the United States obtained the right to establish twenty-two military bases across the archipelago, sites where its forces were free from Filipino legal jurisdiction. In addition, the Filipino economy was closely bound by tariff and currency agreements to the American economy. Elsewhere across the Pacific, the network of island bases that the United States had established during the war became Strategic Trust Territories at its conclusion. These initiatives became the basis for the projection of American power around the world in the postwar era. Its economic and strategic interests were sustained through favorable trade and defense agreements with sovereign states, which were undergirded by a global network of American military bases and a global financial system centered squarely in Wall Street. Colonial control of foreign territories simply became unnecessary.

Chapter 3
A world disordered and reordered

When viewed from the vantage point of the early twenty-first century, what seems most striking about the decolonization of the Third World is the speed and scale of this political storm. It took little more than thirty years from the conclusion of World War II for Western colonial rule over non-Western peoples to come to an end, giving way to well over a hundred new nation-states across the Third World. How did this happen? Those who have studied the subject have identified a number of factors, and their disagreements hinge largely on the relative weight they give to each. Some have emphasized colonial peoples' struggles for independence, arguing that their determined efforts forced imperial overlords into retreat. Others have insisted that the initiative arose from the European powers themselves, which came to regard formal colonial possessions as less relevant to their political and economic agendas. Still others have emphasized the role of outside actors such as the United Nations and the two postwar superpowers, which characterized colonialism as outmoded, even immoral, and exerted diplomatic and ideological pressure to bring it to an end. All of these factors came into play, though they varied in significance by time, place, and circumstance.

It is all but impossible to detail the complex interaction of such varied forces across multiple locations or measure their relative importance from case to case. Causation is complicated, and its particulars matter less for our purposes than participants' own conceptions of its course and outcome. Although we might retrospectively regard decolonization as the near inevitable consequence of great forces, this is not how contemporaries saw it. Both the defenders and opponents of colonial rule believed its fate lay in their hands, and they fought with fierce determination to shape the outcome. From the first phase of decolonization in the late 1940s through its third phase in the 1970s, this epochal transformation was punctuated by a series of violent upheavals, traumatic events that shook the political landscape. Even in places where the transfer of power was peaceful—as it was in a number of colonies—the choices made there cannot be divorced from the speculations, calculations, and concerns that arose from the broader struggle for independence and, in particular, from those contested locations where events would spin out of control.

Strategies of conciliation and coercion

In their determination to hold on to their colonial possessions, imperial authorities had two main options available to them—conciliation and coercion. Both options had been integral to colonial rule from the start, but imperial officials had to recalibrate their relative importance and application in response to the forces that were seeking independence. They engaged in strategies that sought to forge stronger systems of clientage with conservative colonial elites, mitigate discontent among more progressive, westernized subjects with promises of political concessions, and suppress radical dissidents with tough security measures. When faced with armed rebellions, they instituted aggressive counterinsurgency strategies that often involved torture, summary executions, detention without trial, and forced relocations.

All of the imperial powers experimented in varying degrees with new constitutional and political structures after World War II in order to gain or reclaim the allegiance of colonial subjects. The

French recast their empire in 1946 as the French Union, which established a new constitutional relationship between metropolitan France and its colonial possessions. These possessions were reclassified as "overseas territories" and "overseas departments," with citizenship rights granted to a larger portion of their populations, though most remained politically marginalized. The purpose of the Union was to stitch the various components of the French empire together as a grand federation, founded on the liberal promise that it would evolve over time into an association of genuine partners. The problem with this promise for many colonial subjects was that it was continually deferred into an indefinite future, while the problem it posed for the French was that those colonials who did attain citizenship rights could claim resources from the state. These competing agendas made the Union unsustainable.

The Portuguese revamped their empire along similar lines, reclassifying their colonies as "overseas provinces" in 1951 and expanding citizenship rights to selected colonial subjects a decade later. The Dutch developed a postwar scheme to give their empire a constitutional makeover as well, but Indonesian resistance prevented its implementation. In each of these cases, colonial subjects were offered marginally more say in their own affairs, but only within institutional structures that ensured their continued subordination to the imperial center. That, of course, was the point of these political reforms.

The British adopted a somewhat different strategy to maintain their empire. The British Nationality Act of 1948 recognized Commonwealth and colonial peoples as British subjects, although this had less to do with a new vision of imperial integration than it did postwar labor demands. As soon as nonwhite immigrants began to arrive on British shores in substantial numbers, the act began to look increasingly problematic to the public and politicians, who responded with greater restrictions on entry. The immediate postwar years also saw the British Commonwealth enlarged and revamped as a multiracial association to accommodate the newly independent states of India, Pakistan, and Sri Lanka. Although its aim was to maintain some measure of British influence over former colonies, it stood in stark contrast to the French Union. Rather than a plan to establish closer integration of the imperial center and its colonial dependencies, the Commonwealth was an alliance of autonomous sovereign states. Britain's colonies could not be members of the Commonwealth, and the only political outlets available to their indigenous populations came about as a result of reluctantly conceded, incremental reforms, which varied widely from colony to colony.

Perhaps the most striking efforts to restructure the British Empire were the plans to consolidate colonies into regional federations. In form if not in substance, the inspiration for this idea came from the constitutional initiatives that had created the Canadian, Australian, and South African states. Each of these dominions had come into existence by conjoining contiguous, but hitherto separate, colonies into single federated polities. Federation fever swept through British imperial officialdom in the 1950s and 1960s. The first of these federation plans was the ill-fated Malayan Union, which sought to balance the political interests of the territory's Malay, Indian, and Chinese communities. It only lasted a year and a half, collapsing in January 1948 under the weight of ethnic Malay opposition. The British tried again once they had crushed the communist insurgency in Malaya, but this time they took care to work mainly in collaboration with the Malay states' princely elites. The result was the federation that incorporated Malaya, North Borneo, Sarawak, and Singapore in 1963. Although Singapore was expelled two years later, the Malaysian Federation survived, essentially the only one to do so.

Other regional federation plans promoted by the British included the South Arabian Federation, the Central African Federation, the East African Federation, and the West Indies Federation. The East African Federation never made it beyond the drawing board, and none of the others lasted more than a decade. They succumbed in part to the divisive political and ethnic pressures that pulled apart the various peoples who inhabited these artificially conceived polities. Above all, however, they were the victims of the imperial hubris that inspired them. The Central African Federation is a case in point. Founded in 1953, this union of Southern Rhodesia, Northern Rhodesia, and Nyasaland was intended to bolster the political power of the region's white settlers, safeguard British access to its agricultural and mineral resources, and create a strategic counterweight to a South Africa ruled by Afrikaner nationalists. For Africans, who vastly outnumbered whites across the region, the creation of the Central African Federation was regarded as a betrayal of their hopes for independence. Their resistance would eventually lead to the federation's collapse. The same fate awaited other British-sponsored federation plans once local peoples saw through the imperial agendas that informed them.

While imperial rulers attempted to conciliate colonial subjects with their political schemes, they also resorted to coercion. Despite the hardships of the postwar era, European governments channeled a surprisingly substantial portion of their scarce economic resources into rearmament. The onset of the Cold War provided one rationale for this development, but another important purpose was to maintain control of their colonies. The British case is especially noteworthy. Even as the postwar Labour government instituted the ambitious suite of social services at home that came to be known as the "welfare state," it also launched the most costly peacetime rearmament program in British history. One of the challenges it faced with the demobilization of its wartime army was a shortage of troops. Indian independence had cut off access to the subcontinent's vast reservoir of military manpower—"an English barrack in the Oriental seas," in Lord Salisbury's inimitable words—which the British had used for the past century and a half to advance its imperial interests. The Labour government responded in 1948 with the National Service Act, which imposed the first peacetime conscription in British history. It required all young men to complete two years of active military service: nearly 1.5 million did so. Many of them were sent to colonial hotspots. National Service did not come to an end until the early 1960s, by which point Britain's retreat from empire no longer made it necessary.

The Dutch and the French instituted military service requirements for young men to meet the challenges of colonial insurgencies as well. A significant portion of the troops the Dutch deployed in Indonesia between 1946 and 1950 were draftees. The French maintained a "volunteer" army until the mid-1950s, but the manpower demands of the war in Algeria forced them to impose conscription at home.

None of the imperial powers relied exclusively on domestic sources to supply their fighting forces, however. All drew heavily on colonial and other nonmetropolitan sources of manpower. The French deployed half a million men in Indochina between 1945 and 1954. They included 233,000 Frenchmen, 123,000 North Africans, 60,000 West and Central Africans, and 73,000 Foreign Legionnaires (including a large number of German war veterans). Casualties were equally heterogeneous: 18,000 Frenchmen, 15,000 Africans, and 11,000 Legionnaires. Yet the main source of cannon fodder consisted of Vietnamese troops: 46,000 of them died for their colonial masters.

All colonial armies actively recruited subject peoples for military service. Drawn mainly from minority, often marginalized ethnic or tribal groups, these recruits were more likely to remain loyal to imperial authorities than majority populations. Christian Ambonese islanders filled this role for the Dutch in mostly Muslim Indonesia. The French relied heavily on Montagnard tribesmen from Vietnam's central highlands, along with Khmer and other ethnic minorities. The British turned to the Gurkhas of Nepal, the Kamba in Kenya, the Tiv in Nigeria, and a variety of other peoples they fondly characterized as "martial races," which were supposed to be innately well suited for military service.

Much of the regular work of repression—rounding up political agitators, intimidating local supporters, keeping a lid on social unrest—was carried out by the colonial police. The first line of defense came from the local community itself, where individuals could always be found who were willing to wield power in service to the colonial state. Suppressing political protest was as important to their mission as crime prevention and detection. As anticolonial movements grew more powerful, however, imperial authorities increasingly turned to professional personnel whose expertise was transferrable from place to place. This was especially evident in the British colonial empire. The Royal Irish Constabulary, whose members were trained along military lines, became an important recruiting ground for police forces in India, Ceylon, Palestine, and elsewhere. When these territories gained independence, their expatriate policemen quickly obtained employment in other colonies. The deterioration of colonial security after World War II created increased demand for their services. In Malaya, for example, the colonial police force ballooned from 11,000 in 1948 to 70,000 in 1952. Even in British West Africa, where political protests remained relatively peaceful, the colonial police forces nevertheless doubled in size between 1945 and 1956. The British spy agency MI5 trained colonial constabularies to conduct intelligence operations, and colonial laws were amended to allow police to establish paramilitary units and operate outside normal legal channels.

Coercion was integral to colonial rule, and violence was integral to coercion. Yet much of that violence occurred in contexts that did not appear overtly political. Colonial authorities often used military force to crack down on strikes and other labor actions, fearing that the mobilization of workers for economic gains could easily turn into protests for political change. They realized that trade unions and their leaders were capable of becoming an important nexus of anticolonial agitation. Even more unnerving to authorities were those random incidents that resulted in unplanned and unpredictable urban street protests. Fearing that such protests might escalate into serious challenges to the colonial state, they often responded with deadly force. More than 100 Moroccans and 200 Tunisians were killed by French security personnel during unrest in those colonies in 1952. When African protests cast the future of the Central African Federation in doubt, officials in Nyasaland declared a state of emergency and terrorized the local population, using paramilitary forces to burn down houses, impose collective fines, and detain more than 1,300 people without trial. In one incident, police fired on an unarmed crowd, killing twenty and wounding twenty-nine. A government report subsequently condemned the Nyasaland Emergency, calling the colony a "police state."

When confronted with determined resistance to their rule, all of the colonial empires resorted to draconian measures. The result was a series of violent struggles that extended across Asia, Africa, and other regions under European colonial rule. The scale and brutality of these conflicts demand our attention, specifically because they give the lie to the suggestion that the European powers willingly ceded independence to their colonial subjects. They expose aspects of the decolonization process that have too often been dismissed as exceptions to the otherwise peaceful transfer of power.

Wars of decolonization

The initial series of violent struggles against colonial regimes were centered in Asia. While the British had withdrawn from their South Asian possessions with some measure of promptitude and dignity in the aftermath of World War II, the Dutch made a determined effort to restore their rule over the peoples of Indonesia, precipitating a bloody conflict that marked the transition from the first to the second phase of postwar decolonization. From 1946 through 1949, the Dutch conducted a brutal campaign in the archipelago that involved 140,000 troops and a militarized police force of 35,000, including the *Stoottroepen* (Shock Troops), who

5. A large gathering of Javanese men prepared to fight in support of the Indonesian independence struggle in 1945. They are armed with simple staves and sharpened bamboo poles, crude weapons that suggest these are untrained volunteers.

specialized in acts of terror. This campaign is said to have been the largest ever conducted by Dutch forces, and it cost the lives of some 100 to 150,000 Indonesians. It was not enough, however, to keep the East Indies Dutch. The massive military effort drained the Netherland's scarce postwar resources, and its ruthlessness provoked an international backlash. As a result, Indonesian independence, which has been declared in August 1945, finally became a reality in December 1949.

The French conducted an equally brutal campaign in Vietnam in an effort to crush the Viet Minh. Because this anticolonial organization was avowedly communist, the conflict became entangled in the Cold War, with the United States supporting the French while the Soviet Union and the People's Republic of China aided Ho Chi Minh's forces. This prolonged the war and made it deeply destructive. The death toll from the conflict numbered nearly half a million, most of them either Vietnamese fighting to free themselves from French rule or innocent civilians caught in the crossfire. But the crushing defeat of French forces at Dien Bien Phu in 1954 turned the tide in the Viet Minh's favor, finally forcing the French to withdraw from the country.

The British had greater success in their contemporaneous struggle to defeat a communist insurgency in Malaya, though this probably had less to do with a more effective military strategy than with a weaker, more marginalized enemy. The rebels consisted almost entirely of members of Malaya's ethnic Chinese population: few from the majority Malay or Indian communities joined the struggle, and much of the security work at the local level was conducted by the Malayan Home Guard, a force that mushroomed to several hundred thousand. The British forcibly repatriated to China some 10,000 persons suspected of subversive loyalties, while many of their compatriots—more than a million Malay Chinese men, women, and children—were rounded up and resettled in fenced villages, where security patrols prevented the occupants from aiding the rebels. Those who resisted resettlement faced homelessness or worse, since areas of militant activity became free-fire zones, with little distinction drawn between civilian and combatant. British forces—some 40,000 regular army personnel (a combination of British, Commonwealth, East African, and Gurkha troops), more than 60,000 specially trained police, and 300,000 Home Guards—vastly outnumbered the 8,000 or so rebels who fought for the Malayan National Liberation Army. The eventual outcome was hardly in doubt. Even so, the rebels did not surrender until 1960—twelve years after the Malayan emergency had been declared. The British lost little time after proclaiming victory in packing up and sailing home, even though they also made sure that power in the newly independent Malaysian federation was placed firmly in the hands of the conservative Malay sultans who had exerted authority under British suzerainty.

In Asia, the corrosive effects of World War II—and especially the Japanese military occupation—had seriously undermined European colonial authority and created fertile ground for postwar political upheavals. European power was eroding in other regions as well, leading to rebellions that proved as traumatic and tragic as any in Asia. No example looms larger than Algeria—so large, in fact, that it has all but overshadowed other wars of decolonization. Some historians have drawn the conclusion from the Algeria case, especially when considered in conjunction with what occurred in Vietnam, that the French were far more intransigent in their resistance to colonial peoples' struggles for independence than other imperial powers, most notably the British. This claim should be viewed with caution: the British and other colonial empires exhibited a similar intransigence in the face of liberation movements, and they were often no less ruthless in their efforts to crush them.

The Algerian war was, nonetheless, one of the most violent uprisings to occur during the era of decolonization. What made it so were two intractable dilemmas. The first derived from Algeria's constitutional status as an integral part of France. As a result, the Algerian war for independence (1954–62) provoked much the same adamant opposition among many Frenchmen as did the Irish crisis for British unionists. The second dilemma arose from the presence in Algeria of approximately 1.3 million settlers, known as the *pieds noirs* (black feet, referring to their Western-style black leather shoes). Their privileged position as French citizens, combined with their discriminatory treatment of the indigenous Arabs and Berbers, inflamed an already volatile colonial situation, while the threats that the liberation movement posed to their livelihoods and property gave desperation to their determination to see it crushed.

Despite the Sétif massacre in 1945, French authorities had managed for a time to ease tensions in Algeria with promises that more of its Muslim population would obtain citizenship rights and a greater say in their own governance under the newly constituted French Union. But the new order was little better than the old, and resentment turned to revolution in 1954, when the National Liberation Front launched a coordinated series of attacks, first in rural areas, then in the cities, where the Battle of Algiers (1956–57) brought the crisis to a dramatic head. As the revolution spread, the French pumped increasingly numbers of troops into Algeria, eventually exceeding 450,000 in 1956. All told, an estimated 2.5 million French servicemen served in Algeria during the course of the war, and 18,000 lost their lives. The French also relied on large numbers of local recruits, Algerian villagers known as *harkis*, who would pay a heavy price for their collaboration. This was the archetypal "dirty war," involving the use of systematic torture, summary executions, and the large-scale resettlement of civilians. All told, 1–3 million Algerians were forced into protected villages and camps for detainees, and a quarter to half a million others died during the war, either killed in military actions or the victims of famine and disease. Yet the French were unable to suppress or contain the rebellion, and it placed an intolerable strain on domestic political institutions, causing the collapse of the Fourth Republic and the return to power of Charles de Gaulle. Even de Gaulle was unable to salvage French pride and power; he cut his losses by conceding Algeria independence in 1962.

Although the British never confronted a colonial crisis that compared to the Algerian war in scale or consequences for domestic politics, it did conduct a series of brutal counterinsurgency campaigns in a futile effort to forestall decolonization. In addition to Malaya, major military operations occurred in Kenya (1952–56), Cyprus (1955–59), Oman (1957–60), and Aden (1963–67), along with a quasi-colonial conflict with Indonesia over Borneo (1962–66). Most of these wars have left scarcely a trace in Britain's public memory. But they too were "dirty wars," marked by modes and levels of violence that far exceeded what was sanctioned under international law. Largely for this reason, the British took care to characterize their counterinsurgency campaigns as "emergencies," not wars: this terminological distinction allowed them to operate outside international oversight regarding the treatment of prisoners and other conduct that might have otherwise provoked condemnation.

The most serious of these conflicts was the Mau Mau rebellion in Kenya. It originated among the Kikuyu peoples who inhabited those parts of the Kenyan highlands where large tracts of land had been alienated to white settlers. Because the rebellion was as much a civil war among the Kikuyu population as it was a challenge to colonial rule, because it failed to draw much support from the colony's other ethnic or tribal groups, and because it was vilified in the international arena as an atavistic movement of bestial savagery, it should have been relatively easy for the British to crush. But the rebels, who came be to known as the Mau Mau, showed surprising strength and resiliency, forcing colonial authorities to declare martial law and bring in the British Army.

The counterinsurgency operation in colonial Kenya involved 10,000 British soldiers and more than 20,000 police and settler irregulars. Many of the atrocities they committed have only recently come to light. The Royal Air Force carpet-bombed the forests that harbored Mau Mau camps. Most of the Kikuyu population—more than a million people by one estimate—was rounded up and resettled in villages patrolled by Home Guards. Several hundred thousand suspected militants were incarcerated in camps where harsh conditions, including beatings and torture, became commonplace. Over a thousand rebels were hanged—twice the number of Algerians executed by the French. An estimated 20,000 Mau Mau rebels and 100,000 Kikuyu civilians died during the war. As in Malaya, the British proclaimed victory, but it proved a pyrrhic one, especially when word leaked out to the press in 1959 that eleven detainees had been beaten to death in the Hola detention camp. The economic, emotional, and public relations costs of the long campaign to defeat Mau Mau convinced London that the time had come to prepare for the transition of power to African leaders, which finally took place in 1963.

The military campaigns that British forces conducted in other colonial theaters devolved into dirty wars as well. Perhaps the most intractable of these operations occurred in Cyprus, where EOKA, a militant ethnic Greek organization seeking political union with Greece, launched attacks on British forces in 1955. Within a year, the island was occupied by 20,000 British troops, supplemented by a large police force drawn mainly from the minority Turkish community. The Cyprus campaign was one of the most ruthless counterinsurgency campaigns the British carried out during their wars of decolonization, though it is not nearly as well known as the Malayan and Kenyan emergencies. Despite the widespread use of violent coercion by British forces, EOKA endured and forced Whitehall into negotiations. Cyprus gained independence in 1960. It came at the cost of intractable divisions between Greek and Turkish Cypriots.

The collapse of the Belgian Congo presented a very different pattern of decolonization, though one that proved no less violent. When political demonstrations by Africans demanding independence led to riots in Leopoldville in 1959, the colonial military, known as the *Force Publique*, used live ammunition to put down the unrest, killing and wounding as many as five hundred people. This was not, however, the opening salvo in a prolonged campaign to prevent decolonization: Belgian authorities swiftly capitulated to nationalist demands, granting independence to the Congo in 1960. Yet it soon became clear that the Belgians did not believe that their control of Congolese affairs had come to an end. The most notorious demonstration of this view occurred when the Belgian commander of the *Force Publique* informed his African officers: "Before independence = after independence." They mutinied. The security situation

6. Congolese march through the streets of Leopoldville (now Kinshasa) in 1960, celebrating the announcement of their country's impending independence. The prevalence of women in the crowd is an indication of their active involvement in the independence campaign.

quickly deteriorated, tens of thousands of white settlers fled the Congo in panic, secessionist movements broke out in several provinces, foreign powers and mercenary forces of various sorts intervened, and the United Nations dispatched a peacekeeping force to restore order. The violence that accompanied this prolonged period of political instability cost hundreds of thousands of Congolese lives.

Finally, the Suez Crisis of 1956, though hardly the last major upheaval to take place during the second phase of decolonization, was in many respects the tragicomic death knell for European efforts to maintain the imperial order through military interventions of the sort that had once been commonplace, often characterized as "gunboat diplomacy." Abdel Nasser, the charismatic ruler of an independent Egypt, had established himself as a leading spokesman for anticolonial sentiments across the Arab world. Britain grew increasingly worried that Nasser's incendiary radio broadcasts were inspiring the Arab masses to rise up against pro-British regimes across the region. France, in turn, became convinced that Nasser was giving covert assistance to Algeria's revolutionaries. When Nasser nationalized the Suez Canal, Britain and France decided to strike, launching a joint invasion of Egypt under the pretext of a peacekeeping mission after Israel, working in collusion with the two powers, invaded the Sinai Peninsula. This was a major military campaign, involving large-scale air, sea, and land operations. Egyptian cities were bombed, the Egyptian air force destroyed, and Egyptian territory occupied, but Nasser blockaded the Suez Canal by sinking ships in the channel and declared a "people's war" that countered the invaders' strategy. With international opinion rapidly mounting against them, the British succumbed to diplomatic and economic pressure, calling off the campaign with the reluctant acquiescence of the French. In the aftermath of the crisis, Nasser saw his reputation rise exponentially around the Arab world, while Britain's prime minister, Anthony Eden, resigned in disgrace. Harold Macmillan, who succeeded him, drew the obvious lesson from this humiliating blunder. In 1960 he toured Africa, concluding his journey in South Africa, where he gave his famous "Winds of Change" speech, which proclaimed that the time had come to grant independence to colonial subjects.

By the late 1960s, Britain and France retained only a few scattered remnants of their former colonial empires. When the third phase of decolonization began in the 1970s, it centered mainly on Portugal's African colonies. Why Portugal, one of the smallest and weakest of the European colonial powers, was able to resist the pressures that had brought about the decolonization of most of the African continent during the previous phase is difficult to explain, though it probably had something to do with Portugal's neutrality during the World War II and its subsequent isolation under the authoritarian rule of General Salazar, which prevented it from participating in the political and economic developments that transformed the rest of Western Europe in the postwar era. In consequence, it remained sheltered from anticolonial challenges much longer than other empires.

Still, Portugal's African colonial subjects could not help but hear that colonialism was coming to an end across much of their continent. They organized nationalist political movements in Angola, Mozambique, and Guinea-Bissau in the 1960s, but Portuguese colonial authorities ruthlessly suppressed these campaigns for independence. Driven underground, anticolonial activists became more militant, and by the 1970s armed rebellions had broken out across Portuguese Africa. At their height, these insurgencies absorbed the attention of some 200,000 troops, making this the largest military operation in modern Portuguese history.

Portuguese forces used the familiar repertoire of counterinsurgency campaigns: detentions without trial, summary executions, forcible resettlement of civilians, and indiscriminate bombing raids, made even more deadly with the addition of napalm to the arsenal of airpower (an innovation introduced by the Americans during their own effort to crush the communist insurgency in Vietnam). We may never know how many Africans died in these wars, but casualties surely numbered in the hundreds of thousands. The long ordeal did not come to an end until April 1974, when the regime in Lisbon was overthrown in a military coup, itself a consequence of the intolerable social and economic burdens these colonial wars had placed on Portugal and the Portuguese. There was an eerie echo of the Algerian war's corrosive impact on France in these events. The new regime precipitately withdrew Portuguese forces from African soil, causing panicked flight by several hundred thousand white settlers and leaving a power vacuum in the ex-colonies that competing insurgent organizations battled with one another to fill.

One reason Portuguese colonial rule lasted as long as it did was because other white minority regimes clung to power across southern Africa. The collapse of the Central African Federation in 1963 had led to independence for Northern Rhodesia/Zambia and Nyasaland/Malawi, but in Southern Rhodesia (now Zimbabwe) the large white settler community responded to the prospect of black majority rule by supporting its Rhodesian Front government's Unilateral Declaration of Independence (UDI) from Britain in 1965. This was a strange case of settler-driven decolonization in defense of the colonial social order. With Portuguese-ruled Mozambique and Angola and Afrikaner-ruled South Africa and Namibia as neighbors, the renegade regime managed to survive for the next fifteen years in spite of international condemnation and economic sanctions. But once Mozambique and Angola gained independence, sanctions against Rhodesia began to bite and the security situation quickly deteriorated. An increasingly deadly and desperate struggle came to a close with a British-brokered settlement that brought the new state of Zimbabwe into existence in 1980. Namibia would follow suit a decade later, freed from the stranglehold of a South African white regime that itself succumbed to black majority rule in 1994 after a prolonged military struggle.

What characterized each of these wars of decolonization was not simply that Europeans fought hard to keep their colonies, but that they fought dirty: they employed modes and measures of violence that they knew to be beyond the bounds of conventional moral standards, flouting the very norms that they themselves espoused and enshrined in international law. They made widespread use of detention without trial, collective punishment, forced resettlement, torture, mass executions, and more. They did so partly because they considered their enemies uncivilized, even savage, a condition that was thought to negate any need to abide by the moral restraints of conventional warfare. This rationale was deeply rooted in the imperial experience, and it had justified plenty of past atrocities. Europeans' conduct also has to be viewed

7. This "wanted" poster by antiapartheid campaigners in London portrays the Rhodesian prime minister Ian Smith, whose quasi-colonial regime held out against black majority rule until 1980, as a murderer. The text states that "the Smith regime has illegally executed over 150 Africans and its security forces have admitted to shooting dead over 600 unarmed African civilians."

in the context of the catastrophic global war from which they had only recently emerged. That war, too, had been unfettered by most moral or legal restraints, creating a precedent that could easily be turned against colonial rebels.

The problem for the imperial powers was that their nationalist opponents espoused the very principles of freedom and self-determination that they themselves had advocated in their war against the Axis powers. This brought to a head the inherent contradiction of liberal imperialism—that coercive means and liberal ends could not coexist. By instigating such ultraviolent, extralegal measures against their colonial subjects, the European empires exposed the ideological bankruptcy of their own rule. Moreover, their actions attracted increasing scrutiny and condemnation in an international arena that granted unprecedented voice to those newly independent nation-states that had just emerged from colonial subjugation. Using their collective power in the United Nations General Assembly and various UN committees, these countries promoted a new and subversively universal interpretation of human rights, one that came to classify colonialism itself as a violation of those rights.

Finally, the violence that colonial regimes directed against their subjects invariably informed the actions and attitudes of those who struggled against them. Not only did violence beget violence, often causing colonial conflicts to spiral out of control, it also gave rise to the view among some anticolonial intellectuals that true freedom could only come through baptism by blood. The most eloquent and influential proponent of this view was Frantz Fanon, the Martinique-born psychiatrist and spokesman for the Algerian revolution, who argued in *The Wretched of the Earth* (1961) that acts of violence were necessary in order to escape from the psychological shackles of subjugation. Colonialism, he declared, "is violence in its natural state, and it will only yield when confronted with greater violence."

Decolonization by consent

Fanon was clearly wrong: some colonial regimes yielded to their subjects' demands for independence without being coerced to do so by violence. The "greater violence" that wracked Algeria was the exception, not the rule. Even though the preceding account has highlighted those cases where decolonization occurred only after terrible struggles, there are a great many other cases where decolonization came about by consent. What accounts for these differences? How can we measure their relative weight on the scale of history? Some commentators suggest that Europeans were generally willing to peacefully transfer power to colonial subjects, but that on certain occasions they were confronted with problems beyond their control, such as ethnic conflicts, political subversion by agents of the Cold War, and international opinion that stirred up peoples not quite ready for the responsibility of self-governance. Others stress the need to distinguish between the aims and actions of different imperial powers, crediting some (Britain usually headlines this category) with far greater willingness to compromise and concede independence to colonial peoples than others—above all, France. The preceding pages have suggested instead that all of the imperial powers were determined to maintain their colonial empires as long as they could do so and that all of them were prepared to use force to serve that end.

If this is so, how do we explain those cases where decolonization occurred with little or no violence? There are several possible explanations. In some instances, the transfer of power was the consequence of a marriage of convenience between indigenous conservative groups and colonial authorities motivated by a shared fear of revolutionary nationalism. When the British negotiated the transfer of power to Sinhalese elites in Ceylon (Sri Lanka) in 1948, the elephant in the room was the collapse of the British Raj across the Palk Strait. Similarly, the rapid disintegration of British power in Palestine provided much of the impetus for Britain's decision in 1946 to renounce its mandate in neighboring Transjordan and transfer authority to the Hashemite emir who soon proclaimed himself King Abdullah I. The French granted independence in 1953 to royalist regimes in Cambodia and Laos in a preemptive move to prevent the deteriorating situation in Vietnam from spilling over the border and boosting radical forces that might ally with the Viet Minh. Much the same set of considerations informed the decision by France to decolonize Morocco and Tunisia in 1954, which came about in the context of the growing unrest in neighboring Algeria. Farther south, the unraveling of colonial rule in the Belgian Congo in 1959–60, which precipitated white flight and civil war, sent shockwaves across the region, spurring other colonial authorities to speed up plans to transfer power to reliable African partners. Once a colonial regime had begun to break apart under the weight of repression and rebellion, the instability that followed put increased pressure on neighboring regimes to reach accommodations with reliable indigenous elites in order to prevent similar crises. These were tactical decisions, not principled ones.

There are also instances of colonies gaining independence because their imperial overlords simply saw no further reason to keep them. This tended to happen in the latter stages of decolonization, when most of the remaining colonies were too small and weak to cause serious political or security concerns, but were also too marginal to shifting strategic and economic considerations to justify the cost required to keep them. In the 1960s and 1970s, Britain divested itself of a slew of colonies that no longer seemed to merit control. These included the Mediterranean island of Malta (1964), the southern African kingdoms of Lesotho, Botswana, and Swaziland (1966–68), and various Caribbean islands, including Barbados (1966), Grenada (1974), and St. Lucia (1979). By the late twentieth century, what remained of the colonial empires consisted mainly of territories that were considered too small and remote to survive as independent states. The French, for example, retained Reunion and a chain of South Pacific islands. The British still rule St. Helena, Gibraltar, and the Falkland Islands. As the case of the Falklands vividly illustrated during and after its invasion by Argentina in 1982, the residents of these residual possessions are often the most vocal proponents of their continued colonial dependency.

The scramble from empire

All of the European imperial powers made determined efforts in the years after World War II to retain or reclaim their colonial possessions in Asia, Africa, and elsewhere. They poured often scarce postwar resources into these efforts, and they demonstrated a willingness when faced with violent opposition to conduct counterinsurgency campaigns that betrayed the ethical principles that they themselves had enshrined as guidelines for conduct in war. When their campaigns failed and their authority crumbled, the consequence was often a precipitate, chaotic rush to withdraw. The historian Roger Louis has argued that European decolonization was as much a "scramble" as European colonization had been. This term aptly captures the often unplanned, disorderly nature of the imperial retreat. The withdrawal from empire was characterized by two striking developments that often get overlooked in celebratory accounts of decolonization. One was the mass flight of European soldiers, settlers, and other colonial agents, along with many of their non-European collaborators. The other was the outbreak of civil wars, ethnic cleansing, and other forms of political violence as competing regional, religious, linguistic, and other groups sought to shape the territorial dimensions and ethnic composition of new nation-states while they were still up for grabs. Both were by-products of the struggles to turn colonies into nation-states.

Chapter 4
The problem of the
nation-state

The nation-state was both the triumph and the tragedy of decolonization. Its triumph lay in the enshrinement of the principle of national self-determination as the universal norm by which political sovereignty and international relations would henceforth be measured and conducted. A process that had begun with the first wave of decolonization nearly two centuries earlier culminated with the granting of independence to millions of Africans, Asians, and other non-Western peoples who henceforth became the citizens of nation-states. These new states were admitted in turn into the international "family of nations" that was institutionally embodied by the United Nations. At the same time, the tragedy derived from the implementation of the nation-building process, which all too often precipitated conflicts between different ethnic, religious, linguistic, and other cultural groups that sought to shape the new nations in accord with their own interests and identities. Millions of people died in these conflicts and tens of millions were driven from their homes, leaving lasting resentments and antagonisms.

Why was the nation-state the near universal outcome of decolonization? And why was that outcome so problematic? These are crucial questions that require answers, but it is important to point out that the nation-state was hardly the only option available in the era of decolonization. Radically different conceptions of sovereignty and citizenship were bandied about as alternatives to a bankrupt colonial order. Imperial authorities attempted to reimagine and reconfigure their relationships to colonial subjects by proposing varying degrees of self-government within layered systems of sovereignty. These concessions attracted support, at least for a time, from some among the colonies' political classes. While other colonial subjects demanded a complete break from the imperial order, many of them preferred composite states, such as federations, rather than nation-states. Even those who set their sights on the establishment of independent nation-states often disagreed about its territorial and cultural parameters. Decolonization was a complex and contentious process that appeared to offer a range of outcomes.

And yet the nation-state has become the default term of choice for the various states that decolonization brought into being. How did this happen? In order to answer this question, we first need to distinguish between the semantics of this state-building process and its reality. While the modern international order is premised on the universality of the nation-state, many of the polities that are commonly classified as nation-states do not actually meet the definitional criteria of the term. If the nation-state is understood to mean a sovereign state whose territorial boundaries coincide with the cultural boundaries of a particular people—what is often termed ethnonationalism—then more often than not it is honored in the breach. Few countries have culturally or ethnically homogeneous populations, and many are riven by conflicts between different cultural or ethnic groups. This is especially true of those states that came into existence as a result of the decolonization of the European colonial empires. In recent years, political scientists and other scholars have devoted increased attention to the ethnic and cultural fault-lines within modern nation-states. It has been suggested that some countries might more accurately be called "state-nations," meaning states that struggle—often unsuccessfully—to incorporate different ethnic groups. By showing that many contemporary states do not conform to the nation-state as an ideal type, these studies complicate the conventional narrative of decolonization as a linear process that led naturally to the nation-state's triumph.

Anticolonial cosmopolitanism

An oft-overlooked characteristic shared by the leaders of most campaigns for independence from colonial rule was their cosmopolitanism. These individuals were invariably multilingual. Many of them had traveled abroad, often for educational purposes. Some had married across cultures. All of them possessed a sense of worldliness, an understanding of other lands and peoples, which served them well in their struggles against empires.

Consider some notable examples from the British imperial world. Mohandas Gandhi had trained as a barrister in London, where he embraced English customs, dress, and ideas. He then spent more than twenty years in South Africa, practicing law and developing his distinctive strategy of civil disobedience. By the time he returned to India in 1915, he felt a virtual stranger in his motherland and devoted the next few years trying to reacquaint himself with the country.

Gandhi's Indian National Congress colleague, the erudite Jawaharlal Nehru, was educated at the elite English educational institutions of Harrow and Cambridge, followed by legal training at the storied London Inns of Court. Nehru retained a strong appreciation for British and, more broadly, European culture throughout his life. The man who led Kenya to independence, Jomo Kenyatta, went to England in 1929 and did not return home until 1948. In the interim he married an English woman, obtained a doctorate in anthropology from the University of London, visited Moscow, and became active in the pan-African movement. Another figure who fell under the spell of pan-Africanism was Eric Williams, the future prime minister of Trinidad and Tobago, who resided in England from 1932 to 1948 and received a

8. Mohandas Gandhi and his associates pose in front of his South African law office in the early twentieth century. In contrast to later iconic images of Gandhi as a dhoti-wearing Indian ascetic, he appears here as a westernized figure, wearing a three-piece suit, taking pride in his professional accomplishments, and displaying confidence in the liberal promise of British imperial rule.

doctorate in history from Oxford. Kwame Nkrumah, the founding father of independent Ghana (Gold Coast), spent a decade in the United States, where he earned a bachelor's and two master's degrees, followed by several years' residence in Britain, where he too was drawn into pan-Africanist circles.

Many of those who led their countries to independence from French rule followed similar trajectories. Habib Bourguiba, the first prime minister of independent Tunisia, had studied law in France and married a French woman. Ahmed Ben Bella, the revolutionary National Liberation Front leader who became independent Algeria's first president, had played for a French soccer team and served in the French Army from 1936 to 1945, fighting in both France and Italy. Leopold Senghor, Senegal's founding father, had gone to France in 1928 to further his education and forge a career, and it was there that his association with other African expatriates inspired the doctrine of negritude, which held that the blacks or "negroes" of Africa and the diaspora shared a common cultural heritage and racial identity. This francophone version of pan-Africanism inspired Senghor to return to Senegal after the war and press for its integration into a larger political union. If worldliness is measured merely in terms of familiarity with foreign lands, Ho Chi Minh must surely rank first among future leaders of countries that gained independence from France. He lived abroad for thirty years—in France (1911, 1919–23), the United States (1912–13), the United Kingdom (1913–19), the Soviet Union (1924, 1933–38), and China (1924–27, 1931–33, 1938–41), where he married a Chinese woman—before finally returning to Vietnam to oversee its struggle for independence.

The leaders of anticolonial movements in Dutch, Belgian, and Portuguese possessions generally had fewer opportunities to travel and study abroad, yet they too possessed cosmopolitan characteristics. Even though Sukarno never ventured far from his archipelagic homeland, Indonesia's founding father was well educated, fluent in Dutch and the Indonesian languages of Malay, Javanese, Sundanese, and Balinese, and possessed some familiarity with English, German, French, Arabic, and Japanese. Patrice Lumumba, the man who led the Belgian Congo to independence, was similarly limited in his travels, but he spoke French, Swahili, and at least three Congolese languages. Guinea-Bissau's Amilcar Cabral and Angola's Agostinho Neto were among the few Portuguese African subjects who obtained advanced degrees in Lisbon, which is where they met and conceived their campaigns for independence. Such experiences and skills were important aspects of the leadership these individuals exhibited, a leadership that rested in large measure on their appreciation of the scale of their struggle.

Alternatives to the nation-state

These anticolonial cosmopolitans understood that the global span of empires demanded a global network of resistance. They were drawn to doctrines that advanced such networks, and each of these doctrines stood either in opposition to or supersession of the ethnic and territorial constraints of nationalism and its institutional manifestation, the nation-state. Implementing them, however, proved far more difficult than their proponents anticipated.

Anarchism attracted anticolonial activists from Asia to the Americas in the late nineteenth and early twentieth century. It established a global network of revolutionaries whose aim was the overthrow of autocratic regimes, often by targeting their rulers for assassination. For anarchists, any state was inherently imperialistic: hence their wholesale rejection of the state as an oppressive institution. With the outbreak of the First World War, however, anarchism had no answer for the unprecedented increase in the coercive power of the belligerent governments, and its appeal quickly diminished.

The Communist International, or Comintern, which was founded by Soviet authorities in 1919 to promote the cause of world communism, largely supplanted anarchism in the interwar years. It shared anarchism's desire to bring metropolitan and colonial revolutionaries together in a transnational campaign against imperialism, but it operated under the central command of a state, the Soviet Union, whose geopolitical concerns shaped its policies. Although the Comintern was instrumental in the development of a transnational radical movement in the interwar years that gave inspiration and support to some anticolonial activists, it also manipulated and even undermined their efforts when it served Soviet interests. In 1943 Soviet authorities shut down the Comintern, concentrating instead on their own country's survival.

After the war, however, communism as a political doctrine attracted renewed attention from anticolonial activists, especially across Asia. The communists' triumph in China in 1949 inspired opponents of colonial rule in Vietnam, Malaya, and elsewhere to model their movements along similar lines. While communism espoused the cause of anticolonial nationalism, its ideological promise of international solidarity provided a compelling vision of a political future that transcended the territorial constraints of the nation-state. Inklings of that future could be glimpsed in the material assistance some communist insurgencies—most notably the Viet Minh under Ho Chi Minh—received from the People's Republic of China and the Soviet Union. But the Sino-Soviet split in the early 1960s cast serious doubts on communism's ability to supersede national interests, doubts that were subsequently confirmed by conflicts such as the Sino-Vietnam War of 1979. Furthermore, the shadow of communism intensified the suspicion and antagonism that imperial authorities harbored toward colonial nationalists, whom they increasingly characterized as pawns of an international conspiracy directed by Moscow and Beijing. It also made the United States more sympathetic toward its postwar allies' attempts to cling to their colonies, frequently

9. This 1967 Chinese poster portrays African, Asian, and other Third World revolutionaries charging their oppressors. Its title declares that the Chinese "resolutely support the anti-imperialist struggles of the people of Asia, Africa, and Latin America." While some independence movements drew inspiration from communist China, its involvement in these campaigns helped to ensure that the struggle over decolonization became inextricably entwined in the Cold War.

condoning and even contributing to the violent repression of subject populations whose struggles for independence came to be interpreted in terms of Cold War imperatives. Although the transnational appeal of communism proved a compelling one for many colonial insurgents, it came at a heavy cost.

For other critics of colonialism, a more compelling transnational strategy was one that sought to mobilize subject peoples on the basis of broadly construed ethnic, racial, or religious identities. Pan-nationalist movements of various stripes—pan-Africanist, pan-Arabic, pan-Asian, and pan-Islamic, among others—sprang up in the late nineteenth century, when the dramatic expansion of communications and transportation networks made it far more feasible to forge a sense of fraternity across great distances. Most of these movements sought to escape imperial rule, although some pan-ethnic enthusiasms were actually orchestrated by imperial states to further their own expansionist ambitions. This was especially true of the pan-German and pan-Slav movements, which often operated as proxies for Wilhelmian/Nazi Germany and Czarist Russia/Soviet Union in their ideological and geopolitical struggles for dominance in eastern Europe. Similarly, imperial Japan did its best to highjack the pan-Asian movement on behalf of its militarist aims in the 1930s. Despite these manipulations, pan-nationalist movements exerted a powerful appeal for many anticolonial activists.

A good example of this appeal is the pan-African movement, which arose at the end of the nineteenth century. Premised on the conviction that all peoples of African heritage shared common interests and concerns, ranging from colonial exploitation in Africa to racial discrimination throughout the Western world, pan-Africanism sought to mobilize Africans and their diasporic cousins in other continents to collective action. The first Pan-African Congress met in London in 1900, and four more followed between 1921 and 1945. Attendees included numerous leaders of independence struggles in African colonies, such as Kwame Nkrumah, Blaise Diagne, Jomo Kenyatta, and Hastings Banda, as well as prominent members of the diasporic black community, including W. E. B. Du Bois, George Padmore, and Richard Wright.

Pan-Africanists warned against the reproduction of the territorial boundaries that had been created in the colonial scramble for Africa. They feared the balkanization of the continent into small, fragile, hostile states. When the transfer of power took place along exactly those lines, some new African heads of state sought to overcome the constraints they faced by proposing regional federations. Julius Nyerere of Tanzania, Jomo Kenyatta of Kenya, and Milton Obote of Uganda issued a joint declaration in favor of

East African federation. Little came of their high-minded proclamation, however. In West Africa, Nkrumah and Sékou Touré, now leaders of the independent states of Ghana (Gold Coast) and Guinea, actually established a political union in 1958, and neighboring Mali joined them a few years later. Nkrumah hoped this initiative would lay the groundwork for the creation of a United States of Africa, but the fledgling union quickly disintegrated. Time and again, the dynamics of decolonization and national self-interest prevented the pan-Africanists' dreams from being realized.

10. An African summit in Casablanca in 1961 attracted the leaders of various newly independent African countries, including, from left to right, Modibo Keita of Mali, Sekou Toure of Guinea, King Mohammed of Morocco, and Kwame Nkrumah of Ghana. This was one of numerous efforts to overcome the fragmentation caused by the creation of separate nation-states and to forge a pan-African association or even a global alliance of Third World countries.

Much the same thing happened in North Africa and the Middle East, where European imperial encroachments gave rise to pan-Islamic and pan-Arabic sentiments. A nineteenth-century proponent of a pan-Islamic project was the Persian-born Jamal al-din al-Afghani, whose extended sojourns in India, Egypt, Turkey, and elsewhere made him an influential advocate for the collective mobilization of Muslim peoples against the corrosive political and cultural impact of the West. Others would echo his arguments in the era of decolonization, and many continue to do so today. But efforts to forge transnational political unions among Muslim or Arab states proved futile. The most successful attempt was the United Arab Republic, a pan-Arab-inspired union between Egypt and Syria, which came into existence in 1958. Within three years it had collapsed.

Still other colonial activists embraced a very different vision of a transnational future, one premised on greater political freedom within the imperial system itself. This counterintuitive strategy was not as misguided as it might seem. The liberal promise of citizenship was integral to the rhetoric of the British and French empires in particular, and both of them put mechanisms in place that made this promise seem attainable—if only just—to colonial elites. From the mid-nineteenth century through the first decade of the twentieth century, the British had granted self-government to settler colonies in Canada, Australia, New Zealand, and South Africa. By the interwar years, these dominions, as they came to be known, were recognized by the international community as autonomous sovereign states with seats at the League of Nations, yet they simultaneously retained their affiliation to the British Empire as founding members of the British Commonwealth.

This hybrid political system offered an attractive model for many Western-educated colonial subjects who sought self-government. Across British West Africa, members of the educated, urbanized African elite framed their campaigns for political rights in terms of allegiance to the British Empire. A case in point was Joseph

E. Casely Hayford, a prominent Gold Coast lawyer and politician who considered himself both a proponent of local self-government and an ardent empire loyalist. The same was true of many leading Indian nationalists in the early twentieth century, including the young Mohandas Gandhi. They envisioned a self-governing India that would remain within the empire as a Dominion, equal in status to other members of the Commonwealth.

The French adopted a different liberal imperial model, one premised on cultural and political assimilation. It had long granted citizenship rights to some colonial subjects, such as those westernized Africans, known as *évolués*, who lived in the original colonial settlements or communes of Senegal. The right to vote in elections, run for office, and even hold seats in the French Parliament was extended in the late nineteenth and early twentieth centuries to other colonial *évolués*. After World War II, the constitution that created the French Union in 1946 recognized all colonial subjects as French citizens, though it did not grant them equal voting rights. Despite these limitations, this federation with France initially appealed to many colonial leaders. Senegal's Leopold Senghor won election to the French National Assembly, as did some other colonials. Even Ho Chi Minh initially expressed high hopes for this new political order, assuring another French colonial subject in 1947: "There is salvation for all of us in the French Union, and you are lucky because it is an organization based upon the voluntary participation of its members."

Yet liberal imperialism's promises were undermined by colonial racism. Policies that placed racial restrictions on colonial subjects' access to political rights and social opportunities were widespread and pernicious, and they were felt most acutely by those who had most eagerly embraced the promises of empire. It was hardly surprising, then, that the most westernized elites among the colonized often became the West's most formidable foes. The problem was especially apparent in colonies with large numbers of white settlers. The million-plus settlers of Algeria, known as the *pieds noirs* (see chap. 3), adamantly opposed any concessions to the Arab population, fearing the erosion of their own power and privileges. Arab Algerians eventually concluded that imperial citizenship was an empty promise, and many of them turned to armed rebellion. Much the same thing happened in the Dutch East Indies, Portuguese Angola, British Kenya, and most every other colony with a substantial settler population.

One of the best-known examples of a colonial subject's disillusionment with liberal imperialism comes from Gandhi's experience in South Africa. Immediately upon his arrival in 1893, Gandhi discovered that he and his fellow Indian immigrants were regarded by white settlers as intruders and inferiors, ranking little higher on their invidious racial scale than the indigenous African population. For someone who had seen himself and his countrymen as partners in the civilizing mission in Africa, Gandhi was shocked by the discriminatory policies and personal invective directed at Indians. Yet he continued for some time to cling to the conviction that the British imperial state did not share the attitudes and agenda of South Africa's white settlers. This faith was sorely tested as Australia, Canada, and New Zealand also instituted racially restrictive citizenship and immigration policies, designed to defend their self-proclaimed status as "white men's countries." Moreover, it became increasingly apparent that British imperial authorities were quietly colluding in those race policies. Gandhi eventually concluded that India and Indians would never achieve equal partnership in the British Empire. Others came to similar conclusions. It is in this context that W. E. B. Du Bois famously diagnosed "the problem of the twentieth century [as] the problem of the color-line."

The nation-state as triumph

The nation-state had long been a constituent element of transnational blueprints for a postcolonial future, though a subordinate one. It assumed greater importance in its own right as those grander schemes broke down. The idea of the independent sovereign state is often traced to the Westphalian system of international relations that developed in Europe in the mid-seventeenth century, but its associations with nationalism and the nation-state came later, arising out of eighteenth-century notions of popular sovereignty, which presumed the existence of a populace that shared a common will or national identity and inhabited a distinct and contiguous territory. Those who came to see the nation-state as the preferred outcome of their anticolonial struggles were inspired by international precedents and driven by domestic pressures.

The international precedents were the products of the two prior waves of decolonization. The United States' reputation as the first country to make the transition from colony to nation-state made it an especially attractive model to many anticolonial movements. It gained particular prominence toward the end of World War I, when President Woodrow Wilson positioned the United States as the leading proponent of national self-determination. Although the high hopes that anticolonial nationalists invested in Wilson's rhetoric came crashing down when it became clear that he did not consider the peoples of the non-Western world qualified for self-government, the United States' reputation as a country worth emulating was revived by President Franklin Delano Roosevelt, who voiced blunt criticisms of European colonialism and insisted that the Atlantic Charter include the clause that affirmed that "all people have a right to self-determination." Ho Chi Minh, though a self-professed communist, borrowed from the opening lines of the American Declaration of Independence when he declared Vietnamese independence in 1945.

Both world wars resulted in international agreements and institutions that provided important, if often unwitting, precedents for the spread of the nation-state. Despite the betrayal of the anticolonial cause by Wilson and his great power partners at the Paris Peace Conference in 1919, their recognition of the new nation-states that came into existence across central and east Europe established a principle of national self-determination, which proved difficult to contain to the continent. The civilizational rationale they used to deny colonial peoples their freedom looked threadbare in light of the savage bloodletting Europeans had inflicted on one another. The League of Nations' mandate system was meant to rebrand that rationale, giving it an internationalist gloss, but it simply confirmed that national sovereignty was now the sine qua non for admission to the international community. With the creation of the United Nations in 1945, those who campaigned against colonial subjugation found it increasingly necessary to trim their sails to the winds of the nation-state.

The South African Jan Smuts, a key architect of the United Nations, envisioned it as a supra-imperial governing body that granted the great powers disproportionate control over the organization through their permanent seats on the Security Council and sanctioned their rule over peoples deemed incapable of self-governance through a Trusteeship Council—effectively the mandates system redux. But critics of colonialism pointed out that the UN Charter placed an emphasis on nationhood as the standard of sovereignty. The General Assembly became an increasingly powerful forum for anticolonial sentiments, strengthened by the growing number of newly independent member states. Colonialism itself came to be characterized as a violation of the UN's Universal Declaration of Human Rights. By the same token, the right of self-determination as understood in international law came to be interpreted as the right to recognition as a nation-state.

The impetus in favor of the nation-state also came from below. Colonized peoples' calls for political rights and other privileges of citizenship carried greater emotional force and seemed more attainable when cast in terms of their particular place and community than when pan-ethnic identities, the international proletariat, or other diffuse, often abstract associations were privileged. The idea of the sovereign nation-state exerted a more immediate, visceral influence on civil society. It could be cast in terms that mobilized mass support. To a remarkable degree this support included women, who played prominent roles in many campaigns against colonial rule. In India they claimed the right to vote. In Nigeria they rioted in the streets. In Algeria they planted bombs that killed Frenchmen. Across the colonial world, women became active participants in nationalist movements, often working alongside their male counterparts.

While nationalist appeals could inspire the masses, the masses could complicate campaigns to win independence. In order to engage peasants, wage laborers, market women, and other common folk, the cosmopolitan elites who led independence movements had to address their concerns in ways they could understand. It became necessary for anticolonial campaigners to grapple with land, labor, and taxation issues that were located most directly within the colonial realm itself. And it became necessary for them to appeal to local constituencies in their own cultural registers, drawing on their dress, dialect, customary practices, religious symbols, and other modes of meaning in order to attract attention and support. Many Western-educated leaders, for example, abandoned their European suits and stiff collars and adopted traditional garb—the skirt-like *dhoti* by Mohandas Gandhi, the black trousers or *quân* by Ho Chi Minh, and so on—so as to look more like "a man of the people." These political strategies inevitably narrowed the reach of the anticolonial campaigns, reducing them at best to the territorial confines of the colony and the political confines of its state apparatus.

The structural constraints of colonialism itself helped to channel the energies of its opponents toward national rather than pan- and transnational objectives. The transportation and communication infrastructures that anticolonial activists relied upon to reach their supporters and spread their messages—roads, railways, postal systems, newspapers, and so on—were contained for the most part within colonial boundaries. The political and military functionaries who exerted the most direct and decisive force against their campaigns—the headmen, policemen, magistrates, soldiers, and the like—were agents of colonial authorities. Insofar as the anticolonial movement's objective was to acquire control of the institutional levers of power, then the colonial state was its primary target. The payoff that came from its capture was direct and obvious: it included control of revenue, jobs for supporters, and other perks that the leaders of independence movements could ill afford to ignore. But it also placed them in a political straightjacket, limiting their leverage in seeking alternative forms of sovereignty. They acquired vested interests in the bureaucratic institutions, legal structures, and territorial borders that had been put in place by their colonial predecessors. This provided at least the foundations for the making of the nation-state; it also pushed other options off the table.

Colonial boundaries posed another problem. However arbitrary those boundaries might appear in the context of precolonial cultural affiliations or state structures, any effort to redraw them ran the risk of provoking conflict with nationalists in neighboring colonies, who had vested interests of their own. One of the founding principles of the Organization of African Unity, which was established by newly independent African countries in 1963, was the inviolability of the political boundaries these countries had inherited from their imperial predecessors. Colonial boundaries became national boundaries by default.

The nation-state as tragedy

The problem with these efforts to establish nation-states is that they often exacerbated regional, occupational, linguistic, ethnic, and other differences among distinct communities within colonies. All too often the result was civil war, ethnic cleansing, and forced migration. Since the end of the Second World War, conflicts between intrastate ethnic, religious, or racial groups have been far more numerous and caused far more deaths than wars between sovereign states. By one count, there have been 127 civil wars between 1945 and 1999, compared to only 25 interstate wars in the same period. Those civil wars produced 16.2 million casualties, vastly outnumbering the 3.3 million who died in interstate wars. The regions most afflicted by civil war have been Africa, Asia, and other places that passed through the third wave of decolonization. While these conflicts are often blamed on weak or so-called failed states, many of them might more accurately be attributed to the daunting challenge of transforming colonial states, whose boundaries had been arbitrarily imposed by imperial powers, into nation-states, whose members were expected to share a common civic identity. The shape and character of these new states was often up for grabs, with various ethnic, religious, linguistic, and other groups competing to determine the outcome. Widespread disorder and destruction invariably resulted.

When the Indian subcontinent was partitioned into the independent states of India and Pakistan in 1947, it produced one of the bloodiest and most traumatic cases of postcolonial nation-building in the twentieth century. Despite decades of parliamentary commissions, government roundtables, and constitutional blueprints by the British, there was no consensus about the sort of state that would replace the Raj. A variety of groups—Hindus, Muslims, and Sikhs, Bengalis, Punjabis, and Tamils, princes and communists, scheduled castes and tribes and more—jockeyed for position as the British prepared to withdraw. The Indian National Congress and the Muslim League, whose rivalry dominated the political scene, pursued irreconcilable goals, fueling communal violence between Hindus and Muslims that brought British India to the brink of chaos. Partition soon seemed the only solution to the deadlock. Even after the decision was made to establish a separate state for Muslims (but not Sikhs or various other religious or ethnic groups), many of the subcontinent's inhabitants had little understanding of what partition meant. Some had no idea where the new boundaries were and which country they belonged to. Hindu and Muslim extremists launched systematic campaigns of ethnic cleansing against members of the other community. Perhaps as many as a million people were killed, tens of thousands of women were raped, mutilated, and kidnapped, and an estimated 12–20 million refugees were forced to flee their homes, seeking shelter across artificial borders in unfamiliar lands. This was nation-building with a vengeance. It left a lasting heritage of bitterness between India and Pakistan, punctuated by three wars to date, and further secessionist movements, one of them resulting in the creation of Bangladesh.

A similar crisis unfolded in postwar Palestine. Here too a plethora of British white papers failed to resolve the increasingly intractable divide between the mandated territory's Jewish settlers and Arab residents, each demanding a nation-state of their own. As political order and public security disintegrated, the British announced their withdrawal from Palestine, handing over responsibility for resolving the crisis into the hands of the United Nations. It proposed a partition plan that most Jews welcomed, but Arab leaders uniformly rejected. Civil war broke out in late 1947 and concluded with a de facto partition that favored the newly founded state of Israel. Jewish forces consolidated their gains by carrying out the ethnic cleansing of large swathes of territory. This involved the destruction of more than 500 Arab villages, the clearing of Arab neighborhoods in major cities, and the forced migration of some 800,000 Arabs from their ancestral homes. As in South Asia, the resulting resentments and conflicts persist to the present day.

Palestine/Israel was a rarity in one crucial respect: its settler population came out on top. Elsewhere, settlers were the ones most likely to flee from colonies when they became nation-states. The scale and speed of that flight could be staggering. Some 650,000 settlers abandoned Algeria within months of independence, and by the time the exodus had come to an end, 1,380,000 *pieds noirs* had relocated to France and another 50,000 to Spain. When the Dutch lost Indonesia, they had to find room at home for 300,000 expatriates who fled from that newly independent country. Belgium had to absorb 80,000 settlers and 10,000 officials when colonial rule in the Congo collapsed with such stunning speed in 1960. Portugal faced an even more daunting demographic challenge as 500,000 settlers and 200,000 troops retreated to its shores after its African empire imploded. All told, some 5.4–6.8 million settlers, officials, and soldiers returned in Western Europe from former colonies in the decades after the Second World War.

As the largest of the European colonial empires, Britain had the greatest pool of potential refugees with racial claims on the mother country. Yet the size and diversity of the empire gave these uprooted colonials a range of choices, minimizing the numbers who returned to British shores. Many of those who fled from India in 1947 found refuge in African colonies or the Australasian dominions. As decolonization spread across West and East Africa, whites who found these newly independent countries unwelcoming often turned instead to Rhodesia or South Africa, where the climate and culture better suited their tastes. And the larger Anglophone world, including the United States and Canada, attracted many others.

If Britain avoided a massive influx of white colonial refugees, it was not untouched by the broader demographic upheavals that decolonization produced. Various diasporic and minority communities who had established niches within colonial economies became the targets of nativist violence. These included tens of thousands of South Asians who were driven out of newly independent East African countries and sought refuge in Britain, where their arrival spurred efforts to reverse the principles of the British Nationality Act and restrict the immigration of nonwhite peoples. There were plenty of other victims of nation-building projects. Burma's Hindu, Muslim, and tribal communities found their positions deteriorate dramatically as the Buddhist majority consolidated its control of that country. Hundreds of thousands of Sephardic Jews were expelled from many newly independent Arab countries. The Lebanese who had established enclaves in colonial West Africa found themselves no longer welcome. The Ambonese Christians who had assisted the Dutch colonial regime as military auxiliaries were forced to flee Indonesia. But no group paid a higher price for choosing the wrong side in the wars of decolonization than the *harkis*, Algerians who collaborated with French military authorities. When Algeria won independence, an estimated 100,000 of them were slaughtered by the victors, while another 100,000 or so escaped to France, where they were incarcerated in refugee camps until the 1970s. Neither postcolonial regimes nor ex-imperial powers offered a place for such peoples.

The larger challenge facing many newly independent states was to find ways to forge a shared sense of national identity among peoples who had viewed one another as antagonists in the past or whose differences had intensified in the course of their political mobilization against colonial rule. This challenge was especially apparent in Africa, partly because colonial boundaries bore so little relation to precolonial political and ethnic sodalities and partly because colonial authorities failed for the most part to establish strong state institutions. Kwame Nkrumah insisted that "there should be no reference to Fantis, Ashantis, Ewes, Gas, Dagombas, 'strangers,' and so forth, but that we should call ourselves Ghanaians—all brothers and sisters, members of the same community—the state of Ghana. For until we ourselves purge from our own minds this tribal chauvinism and prejudice of one against the other, we shall not be able to cultivate the wider spirit of brotherhood." These were noble sentiments, but they were rarely realized. Newly independent states all too often disintegrated into civil war.

In the Congo, an army mutiny in 1960 caused the sudden collapse of the Belgian colonial regime, but the nationalist government that came to power immediately faced secessionist movements in several parts of this vast central African country. The crisis was made worse by the rivalry between the Cold War superpowers and self-serving interference by foreign mining companies, and it resulted in intervention by a UN peacekeeping force, an American-supported coup against Patrice Lumumba, which resulted in his murder, and other complicating events. A military dictatorship eventually restored some semblance of central authority in 1965, although civil conflicts continue to plague the country and kill millions of people.

Other notable postcolonial civil wars occurred in Nigeria, Angola, and Sudan. Seven years after Nigeria won independence from Britain in 1960, long-simmering ethnic tensions led to a secessionist movement by the Igbo people who occupied the country's southeast region. The resulting Biafran war left a million dead. Angola's civil war started as soon as Portuguese rule collapsed in 1975, and it continued for several decades. It pitted the two leading liberation movements against one another, each drawing support from different regions of the country where different ethnic groups predominated. Half a million Angolans died in the war and millions more were displaced. Our third example, Sudan, has been racked repeatedly by civil war since its independence in 1955. One major line of fracture has been the Muslim north versus the animist and Christian south. Over the decades, war and famine have resulted in several million deaths. With the creation of South Sudan in 2011, this is a rare instance of a civil war in postcolonial Africa resulting in an internationally recognized secession. Almost nowhere else have the struggles between contending parties altered the territorial boundaries inherited from the colonial era. Instead, Africans have sought with varying degrees of success to forge nations from the mix of peoples that colonialism had joined in single states.

The consequences of the Cold War

Many of these conflicts were worsened by the Cold War rivalry between the United States and the Soviet Union. The two superpowers and their allies supported rival parties in their struggles to wield influence over postcolonial states, supplying them with money, weapons, and military advisors. Their involvement invariably enlarged, intensified, and prolonged hostilities, and civilian populations suffered accordingly. African examples include the Angolan conflict, exacerbated by the intervention of Cuban and South African troops as proxies for Soviet and American interests, and the Horn of Africa, where territorial disputes between Ethiopia and its neighbors were made more deadly as a result of involvement by the superpowers.

The most serious crises to arise from this convergence of local and global conflicts occurred in East Asia, where the outcome of decolonization carried particularly high stakes for the Cold War. Korea and Vietnam were the principal flashpoints. In both cases, the problem had less to do with ethnic or other cultural divisions bubbling up from below than political divisions being imposed from above. Even under Japanese colonial rule, the Korean population had possessed a strong sense of national identity, but the postwar occupation of the northern half of the peninsula by Soviet forces and the south by American forces forestalled political unification. North Korea's effort to force the issue by invading the south in 1950 precipitated a war that cost millions of lives and left Korea permanently divided. In Vietnam, the Geneva Accords that established the terms for the French withdrawal in 1954 stipulated the temporary partition of the country, but Cold War rivalries hardened this division and drew the United States into a long and devastating war in defense of a separate South Vietnam. In contrast to the Korean case, however, this struggle ended in 1975 with reunification when American forces withdrew from the conflict and North Vietnam overwhelmed its southern neighbor.

The Cold War provides the conventional framework for explaining the involvement of the United States and the Soviet Union in these upheavals, but there is another way to interpret their interference. If the two superpowers are understood to be empires, then the meddling role they played in unstable new countries echoes the actions of other empires after earlier waves of decolonization. To be sure, neither the American nor the Soviet empire resembled those that disintegrated in the decades after World War II. Both of them condemned colonialism as incompatible with their ideological principles and both eschewed opportunities to impose direct imperial rule over other peoples, at least for the most part. In a world of nation-states, colonial empires no longer made sense. The United States and the Soviet Union developed new modes of power that provided their dependencies at least the pretense of national sovereignty. And even though they occasionally intervened directly in the affairs of other countries, they more often employed proxies or exerted indirect forms of pressure to achieve their aims. The third wave of decolonization, then, did not make empires obsolete; it merely modified their methods.

Chapter 5
Imperial continuities and the politics of amnesia

The collapse of the colonial empires and the rise of new nation-states together comprise one of the great transformations in modern history. The world we inhabit today is profoundly different in its geopolitical character from the one that existed in the mid-twentieth century. At that time, millions of the earth's inhabitants were still governed against their will by foreign imperial powers. Now nearly all peoples are citizens of states that ostensibly embody their national will. The significance of this transformation in the global political order cannot be denied.

At the same time, it is important to acknowledge and examine the continuities between the colonial past and the postcolonial present. Those continuities can be discerned at multiple levels. They have informed political agendas and economic policies in the Third World, as well as the First. They have colored ideological and cultural debates in both regions. They have animated the recent recovery of painful, long buried memories on the part of ex-imperial and ex-colonial peoples alike. And they have recapitulated the past in the present with the breakup of the Soviet Union, reminding us that the phenomenon we have characterized as decolonization is a recurrent process.

Neocolonialism and nonalignment

The individuals who led their countries to freedom from colonial rule were acutely aware of the limits of national independence. They established authority over countries that were highly fragile, often riven by domestic discord, and usually burdened by weak economies and unfair terms of trade. Ghana's Kwame Nkrumah, one of the most astute of these new leaders, coined the term "neocolonialism" to refer to the way the West continued to exerted considerable sway over ex-colonies. Other terms that gained currency to describe this state of affairs were dependency and underdevelopment. They placed particular emphasis on the economic constraints that confronted new countries, limiting their access to international markets and capital and relying on systems of clientage that favored ex-imperial rulers.

Perhaps the most striking example of neocolonialism has been France's relationship with its former colonies in West and Central Africa. Known as *la Francafrique*, this relationship has been characterized by the motto *"partir pour mieux rester"* (leave in order to remain). For decades the African countries that had been French colonies continued to peg their currency to the French franc and deposit most of their reserves in the French treasury. Their natural resources continued to be extracted under sweetheart contracts with French companies, while French experts continued to exert inordinate influence over their businesses and bureaucracies. France retained control of military bases across the region and used the troops they stationed there to intervene in the domestic political affairs of host countries. Since 1960, the French have undertaken more than twenty military actions in the region, keeping cooperative regimes in power and overthrowing less pliant ones.

Although newly independent countries elsewhere across the Third World endured military interventions by their ex-imperial masters—the most dramatic and disastrous case in point being the joint British-French invasion of Egypt to reclaim the Suez Canal in 1956—the more prevalent form of postcolonial coercion came from international organizations like the International Monetary Fund and the World Bank, both of which imposed socially destructive monetary policies on poor countries in return for financial assistance. Moreover, many of the technical experts who came to these countries to oversee development projects under the auspices of the United Nations, nongovernmental organizations (NGOs), and other ostensibly independent agencies were ex-colonial officials, often imbued with the prejudices and paternalism of the past.

In an effort to escape the economic and political influence of their neo-imperial overlords, the leaders of these ex-colonial states sought to forge transnational alliances with one another. These efforts echoed earlier calls for regional federations and pan-ethnic projects. The most noteworthy of these attempts to bring together countries that shared a history of colonial subjugation was the Bandung Conference, which drew representatives from twenty-five African, Asian, and Middle Eastern countries to Indonesia in 1955. The conference condemned colonialism "in all of its manifestations" (implicitly objecting to its practice by the Soviet Union as well as the Western powers) and issued a high-minded declaration of the participants' shared desire for economic cooperation, human rights, and world peace. It generated little in the way of practical initiatives, however. Even so, Bandung announced the arrival on the international scene of a new geopolitical entity, which soon came to be known as the Third World. It was followed by two Afro-Asian Peoples' Solidarity Conferences (1957, 1961), an All-African Peoples Conference (1958), and the formation of the Non-Aligned Movement (1961). Member nations, however, found it difficult to extricate themselves from the constraints of the Cold War and forge common ground across the gulf of sovereign self-interest and ideological division. Perhaps the most successful strategy for escaping these forces was the economic alliance of oil-producing nations, OPEC, composed mainly of postcolonial states from the Middle East, Africa, and Southeast Asia. In 1973 it managed to bring the Western economies to their knees during the oil embargo.

Another route of resistance involved the rejection of Western values and ways of life. This approach also had a long lineage, one that was deeply rooted in indigenous cultural traditions and their reassertion under colonial rule. In India, for example, both Mohandas Gandhi and Rabindranath Tagore made use of those traditions to condemn Western industrial civilization as excessively materialistic, with Gandhi damning it in his book *Hind Swaraj* (1909) as a disease. The postcolonial version of this critique sought to escape the ideological and epistemological influence of the West. The Kenyan novelist Ngugi wa Thiong'o urged his countrymen to reject Western languages and embrace indigenous vernaculars, arguing in *Decolonising the Mind* (1981) that the psychological liberation of ex-colonial peoples depended on it. The rise of postcolonial studies, which came to prominence in the aftermath of the Cold War and economic globalization in the 1990s, also can be viewed as an attempt to challenge the epistemological predominance of Western modes of thought and forge a sense of shared identity derived from the colonial experience.

While postcolonial states found it difficult to extricate themselves from their colonial pasts, their postimperial counterparts seemed to make remarkably painless transitions to a world without colonies. Granted, the flood of refugees from ex-colonies placed pressure on the metropolitan countries to which they claimed membership, and in at least two cases the pressures posed by decolonization caused major political crises at home: the Algerian conflict brought about the collapse of the French Fourth Republic in 1958, and the strains of the counterinsurgency campaigns in Africa precipitated the military coup that overthrew Portugal's autocratic regime in 1974. Yet the more significant story is the speed with which European countries recovered from the loss of their empires. France, for example, found a new raison d'etre in the European Economic Community, which eventually became the European Union. While never entirely retreating from those parts of the world they had once ruled, they established an economic and political alliance among one another that provided, at least until recently, a highly successful alternative to empire.

Memory and forgetting

In his 1882 lecture "What is a Nation?" the French historian Ernest Renan observed: "Forgetfulness, and I would even say historical error, are essential in the creation of a nation." This was necessary, he argued, because nations are forged through campaigns of "extermination and terror" that must be forgotten or obscured by fictive histories if they are to overcome their bloody origins and endure. Renan was reflecting on the violent birth of the French nation, but his penetrating insights seem even more pertinent to the postcolonial histories of nation-building that have followed.

Until recently, most accounts of the partition of British India focused on high politics, examining the calculations and negotiations that took place between Viceroy Mountbatten, the Indian National Congress leaders Gandhi and Nehru, and the leader of the Muslim League, Muhammad Jinnah—an important subject but one that overlooked the experiences of millions of common people whose lives were turned upside down in the Punjab and Bengal. The only way many of them managed to cope with the maelstrom of partition, and the physical and emotional trauma it inflicted, was by willfully retreating into a state of amnesia. The states of India and Pakistan/Bangladesh abetted this amnesia through their celebratory histories of independence. Over the past decade or so, historians, filmmakers, playwrights, and others have begun to break through the barrier of distance and denial, recovering and recording the long-suppressed memories of partition's survivors. Oral history projects, social histories, and other initiatives have brought the manifold personal scars of partition back into the public arena, provoking debate and moral reflection.

Most postcolonial countries have not gone quite so far in revisiting the painful circumstances of their creation. The emotional scars often remain too raw, the political repercussions too great. Some regimes are simply too insecure to countenance such inquiries. In other cases, the communities that paid the heaviest price for these nation-building projects are no longer present to pose troubling questions. Many Palestinian villages that once existed in what is now Israel, for example, have become forests, parks, and other open spaces, erasing the existence of their prior inhabitants from public memory. The truth and reconciliation commissions that have proliferated in many countries in recent years have for the most part focused on more recent political traumas, but the South African commission, which served as a model for many others, sought to come to terms with the crimes that accompanied the struggle over black majority rule, a war of decolonization in all but name.

For the European countries that had ruled so much of the world, the memories of their imperial past were invariably given a nostalgic glow by popular culture. Yet the traumas of decolonization have recently come back to haunt these states and their citizens. The unseemly side of imperial retreat has been exposed in a number of public controversies and legal cases. In 2000, *Le Monde* published an Algerian nationalist woman's shocking account of the torture she had suffered at the hands of French forces in their campaign to crush the revolution. The story led to further revelations of torture, assassination, mass internment, and other abuses, spawning a wrenching national debate about French conduct during this dirty war. In 2011 and 2013, Dutch courts ruled that its soldiers had massacred hundreds of innocent civilians in two separate villages during Indonesia's struggle for independence, resulting in an official apology by the Dutch government to the Indonesian people, as well as financial compensation for the victims' surviving widows. This was part of a broader effort by lawyers, historians, and others in the Netherlands to expose the war crimes committed by Dutch forces during that bloody struggle. And in 2012, London's High Court ruled that a lawsuit filed on behalf of four elderly Kenyans, who were seeking damages for the torture they endured at the hands of colonial forces during the Mau Mau rebellion, had merit and could proceed. This led the British government to reach an out-of-court settlement that provided £20 million in compensation to the plaintiffs and another 5,225 living Kenyans who had been victims of similar abuse. The impetus for this action was the stunning discovery that the government had a secret cache of files confirming that authorities in Whitehall had sanctioned torture and other extralegal activities during the Kenyan emergency. Moreover, these files comprised only a small

11. These four elderly Kenyan plaintiffs successfully sued the British government for torturing them during the Mau Mau rebellion. The landmark 2012 case offers dramatic evidence of the lingering afterlife of empire.

portion of the politically explosive records concerning the end of empire that authorities had kept hidden from public view. As these records are made available for public examination, they will no doubt spark more controversies and reassessments of British decolonization.

Imperial continuities

Lest we conclude that empires had become a thing of the past and that the traumas of decolonization are merely matters of distant memory, the story does not end with the third wave of decolonization. As the European colonial empires crumbled in the decades after World War II, the United States and the Soviet Union picked up the pieces, forging new empires that exerted influence over a variety of other states and societies during the decades of the Cold War. And when the collapse of the Soviet Union brought the Cold War to an abrupt end, it also precipitated a new wave of decolonization. The Soviets never possessed a conventional colonial empire, but they certainly exerted quasi-colonial control over the many non-Russian peoples and regions that had been incorporated within the Soviet Union and subjected to autocratic rule from Moscow. Moreover, the Soviets installed puppet regimes in the East European states that came under their sway after World War II, and they suppressed rebellions in East Germany in 1953, Hungary in 1956, and Czechoslovakia in 1968 with much the same ruthless determination as did the French and the British in various parts of their empires.

Like prior waves of decolonization, the decolonization of the Soviet empire can be viewed as a repercussion of a global war between empires. Even though the Cold War did not draw the Soviet Union and the United States into a devastatingly direct military confrontation, it did involve them in a worldwide struggle that placed immense pressure on their economic resources and institutional structures. For the Soviets, the decade-long war in

Afghanistan (1979–89) proved too much to bear, precipitating the political collapse of the communist regime, which led in turn to the disintegration of its empire.

This fourth wave of decolonization involved several distinct, though related, developments. One was the restoration of independence to those central and eastern European nation-states that had originally come into existence after World War I. Albania, Bulgaria, Czechoslovakia, Estonia, Hungary, Latvia, Lithuania, Poland, Romania, and Yugoslavia reclaimed the political autonomy they had all lost in varying degrees to the Soviet Union. A second development was the breakup of the Soviet Union itself in 1991, which permitted those "republics" that had been incorporated as constituent elements of the Soviet state after World War I to claim sovereignty as the independent countries of Armenia, Azerbaijan, Belarus, Georgia, Kazakhstan, Kyrgyzstan, Tajikistan, Turkmenistan, Ukraine, and Uzbekistan. As the states that arose from the ruins of the Soviet empire undertook nation-building projects, they became embroiled in debilitating conflicts. Territorial disputes broke out between neighboring states, and violent clashes occurred between different ethnic, religious, and linguistic groups within states. Armenia and Azerbaijan, for example, went to war over a region claimed by each of them. Ethnic violence broke out in Georgia, Tajikistan, and various other newly formed countries. Elsewhere, especially in central and eastern Europe, states dissolved into smaller, more ethnically homogeneous entities. This process took place peacefully in the case of Czechoslovakia, which separated into the Czech Republic and Slovakia, but it generated a prolonged and bloody struggle over the future of Yugoslavia, which eventually fragmented into Croatia, Kosovo, Macedonia, Montenegro, Serbia, and Slovenia. All too often, these upheavals bore all the hallmarks of the disorder that had accompanied earlier waves of decolonization.

Aggravating these problems were Russia's tenacious efforts to maintain and recover portions of its empire. Like so many of the empires that preceded it, Russia was reluctant to release its grasp of subject peoples and territories. It fought ferociously to retain control over Chechnya and neighboring Muslim-majority regions of the Caucasus. It went to war against Georgia. It annexed the Crimea from Ukraine and encroached on its eastern provinces. These and other aggressive actions suggest that it has still not come to terms with the loss of its empire.

The United States, in turn, attained a level of global supremacy in the aftermath of the Soviet collapse that many commentators considered historically unprecedented. The French foreign minister coined the term "hyperpower" to communicate its special standing in world affairs. Others have pointed out that America's military budget exceeds that of the next ten to twelve most powerful nations combined, and that it maintains more than a thousand military bases and other security installations around the globe. In the estimation of many observers, America's ability to project its power almost anywhere in the world surely qualifies it as an empire. But it is certainly not a colonial empire, though it does exert quasi-colonial authority over such scattered territories as Puerto Rico and Guam. The question, then, is whether the collapse of this empire, which will surely come sooner or later, will produce something like a fifth wave of decolonization?

References

Introduction

UN General Assembly Resolution 1514 (XV), December 14, 1960: "Declaration on the Granting of Independence to Colonial Countries and Peoples" at http://www.un.org/en/decolonization/declaration.shtml

Clement Attlee, *Empire to Commonwealth* (London: Oxford University Press, 1961), 1.

Chapter 1: Waves of decolonization

American Declaration of Independence at http://www.archives.gov/exhibits/charters/declaration_transcript.html

Mariano Mareno quoted in Jeremy Adelman, *Sovereignty and Revolution in the Iberian Atlantic* (Princeton, NJ: Princeton University Press, 2006), 215.

Vladimir Lenin, *Imperialism: The Highest Stage of Capitalism* (1917), preface to the French and German editions, at https://www.marxists.org/archive/lenin/works/1916/imp-hsc/

Erez Manela, *The Wilsonian Moment: Self-Determination and the International Origins of Anticolonial Nationalism* (New York: Oxford University Press, 2009).

Chapter 2: Global war's colonial consequences

Timothy Snyder, *Bloodlands: Europe Between Hitler and Stalin* (New York: Basic Books, 2010).

Churchill comment in Archibald Wavell, *Wavell: The Viceroy's Journal*, ed. Penderel Moon (Karachi: Oxford University Press, 1997), 120.

Dato Onn bin Ja'afar quoted in John Keay, *Last Post: The End of Empire in the Far East* (London: John Murray, 2000), 230.

Brazzaville statement quoted in D. Bruce Marshall, *The French Colonial Myth and Constitution-Making in the Fourth Republic* (New Haven, CT: Yale University Press, 1973), 107.

Keynes quoted in L. J. Butler, *Britain and Empire: Adjusting to a Post-Imperial World* (London: I. B. Tauris, 2002), 61.

Chapter 3: A world disordered and reordered

Frantz Fanon, *The Wretched of the Earth*, trans. Constance Farrington (New York: Grove Press, 1963), 61.

Wm. Roger Louis, *Ends of British Imperialism: The Scramble for Empire, Suez, and Decolonization* (London: I. B. Tauris, 2006).

Chapter 4: The problem of the nation-state

Ho Chi Minh quoted in Sophie Quinn-Judge, "Ho Chi Minh: Nationalist Icon," in *Makers of Modern Asia*, ed. Ramachandra Guha (Cambridge, MA: Belknap Press, 2014), 74–75.

W. E. B. Du Bois, *The Souls of Black Folk* (New York: New American Library, 1969), Forethought.

Kwame Nkrumah, *I Speak of Freedom: A Statement of African Ideology* (New York: Frederick A. Praeger, 1961), 168.

Chapter 5: Imperial continuities and the politics of amnesia

Ernest Renan, "What is a Nation?" at http://ucparis.fr/files/9313/6549/9943/What_is_a_Nation.pdf

Further reading

The scholarship on decolonization has grown at an increasingly rapid pace in recent years, reflecting a renewed interest in the subject and reassessments of its legacies. Among the general resources that readers will find useful are Dietmar Rothermund, *The Routledge Companion to Decolonization* (London: Routledge, 2006), which is a rich compendium of information, and three "readers": Todd Shepard, *Voices of Decolonization: A Brief History with Documents* (Boston: Bedford/St. Martin's, 2015); Prasenjit Duara, ed., *Decolonization: Perspectives from Now and Then* (London: Routledge, 2004); and James D. Le Sueur, ed., *The Decolonization Reader* (London: Routledge, 2003). For informative narrative accounts of the subject, see Martin Shipway, *Decolonization and Its Impact: A Comparative Approach to the End of the Colonial Empires* (Oxford: Blackwell, 2008); Michael Burleigh, *Small Wars, Faraway Places: Global Insurrection and the Making of the Modern World, 1945–1965* (New York: Viking Penguin, 2013); Martin Thomas, Bob Moore, and L. J. Butler, *Crises of Empire: Decolonization and Europe's Imperial States, 1918–1975* (London: Hodder Education, 2008); and Martin Thomas, *Fight or Flight: Britain, France, and Their Roads from Empire* (Oxford: Oxford University Press, 2014). Odd Arne Westad's magisterial *The Global Cold War* (Cambridge: Cambridge University Press, 2007) tells much the same story from a Cold War perspective.

Regarding what chapter 1 refers to as the first two waves of decolonization—those that occurred in the New World and the Old World—the following works are especially helpful: Jeremy Adelman, *Sovereignty and Revolution in the Iberian Atlantic* (Princeton, NJ:

Princeton University Press, 2006); Erez Manela, *The Wilsonian Moment: Self-Determination and the Origins of Anticolonial Nationalism* (New York: Oxford University Press, 2009); Eric D. Weitz, "From the Vienna to the Paris System: International Politics and the Entangled Histories of Human Rights, Forced Deportations, and Civilizing Missions," *American Historical Review* 113, no. 5 (December 2008): 1313–43; and, more generally, David Armitage, *The Declaration of Independence: A Global History* (Cambridge, MA: Harvard University Press, 2007) and Mark Mazower, *Governing the World: The History of an Idea, 1815 to the Present* (New York: Penguin, 2012). Also important is Susan Pedersen, *The Guardians: The League of Nations and the Crisis of Empire* (New York: Oxford, 2015).

Key works on the decolonization of specific empires and colonial territories include: L. J. Butler, *Britain and Empire: Adjusting to a Post-Imperial World* (London: I. B. Tauris, 2002); Benjamin Grob-Fitzgibbon, *Imperial Endgame: Britain's Dirty Wars and the End of Empire* (Houndsmill: Palgrave Macmillan, 2011); Christopher Bayly and Tim Harper, *Forgotten Wars: Freedom and Revolution in Southeast Asia* (Cambridge, MA: Belknap Press, 2007); Yasmin Khan, *The Great Partition: The Making of India and Pakistan* (New Haven, CT: Yale University Press, 2007); John Keay, *Last Post: The End of Empire in the Far East* (London: John Murray, 2000); Wm. Roger Louis, *The British Empire in the Middle East 1945–1951: Arab Nationalism, the United States, and Postwar Imperialism* (Oxford: Clarendon Press, 1984); Alistair Horne's classic *A Savage War of Peace: Algeria, 1954–1962* (New York: New York Review Books, 2006 [1977]); Frederick Cooper, *Citizenship Between Empire and Nation: Remaking France and French Africa, 1945–1960* (Princeton: Princeton University Press, 2014); Todd Shepard, *The Invention of Decolonization: The Algerian War and the Remaking of France* (Ithaca, NY: Cornell University Press, 2006); David Anderson, *Histories of the Hanged: The Dirty War in Kenya and the End of Empire* (New York: W. W. Norton, 2005); Caroline Elkins, *Imperial Reckoning: The Untold Story of Britain's Gulag in Kenya* (New York: Henry Holt, 2005); and Norrie MacQueen, *The Decolonization of Portuguese Africa: Metropolitan Revolution and the Dissolution of Empire* (London: Longman, 1997).

On the problems of nation-building, ethnic violence, and forced migrations, see Karen Barkey and Mark von Hagen, eds., *After Empire:*

Multiethnic Societies and Nation-Building (Boulder, CO: Westview Press, 1997); Caroline Elkins and Susan Pedersen, eds., *Settler Colonialism in the Twentieth Century* (New York: Rutledge, 2005); Panikos Panayi and Pippa Virdee, eds., *Refugees and the End of Empire: Imperial Collapse and Forced Migration in the Twentieth Century* (London: Palgrave, 2011); Ilan Pappe, *The Ethnic Cleansing of Palestine* (Oxford: Oneworld, 2007); Jeffrey Herbst, Terence McNamee, and Greg Mills, eds., *On the Fault Line: Managing Tensions and Divisions Within Societies* (London: Profile Books, 2012); Fabian Klose, *Human Rights in the Shadow of Colonial Violence: The Wars of Independence in Kenya and Algeria* (Philadelphia: University of Pennsylvania Press, 2013); and Ramachandra Guha, ed., *Makers of Modern Asia* (Cambridge, MA: Belknap Press, 2014). For an interesting inquiry into the relationship between imperial decline and decolonization, see Alfred W. McCoy, Josep M. Fradera, and Stephen Jacobson, eds., *Endless Empire: Spain's Retreat, Europe's Eclipse, America's Decline* (Madison: University of Wisconsin Press, 2012).

Finally, those who took part in struggles for independence from imperial rule wrote books that remain well worth reading. Two of the most important are M. K. Gandhi, *Hind Swaraj* (Cambridge: Cambridge University Press, 1997 [1910]) and Franz Fanon, *The Wretched of the Earth* (New York: Grove Press, 2005 [1961]). Also enlightening are Richard Wright, *The Color Curtain: A Report from the Bandung Conference* (Jackson: University Press of Mississippi, 1995 [1956]); Kwame Nkrumah, *I Speak of Freedom: A Statement of African Ideology* (New York: Frederick A. Praeger, 1961); and Ngugi wa Thiong'o, *Decolonising the Mind* (London: Heinemann, 1986). A useful overview of anticolonial thought is Margaret Kohn and Keally McBride, *Political Theories of Decolonization: Postcolonialism and the Problem of Foundations* (New York: Oxford University Press, 2011).

Index

Index